# Braxton's Practical Cook Book

# Prepared for Economy, Family and Hotel Use

by G. F. Braxton

WESTPHALIA PRESS
An Imprint of Policy Studies Organization

Westphalia Press
An imprint of Policy Studies Organization
1527 New Hampshire Ave., NW
Washington, D.C. 20036
info@ipsonet.org

ISBN-13: 978-1-63391-585-5
ISBN-10: 1-63391-585-9

Cover design by Jeffrey Barnes:
jbarnesbook.design

Daniel Gutierrez-Sandoval, Executive Director
PSO and Westphalia Press

Updated material and comments on this edition
can be found at the Westphalia Press website:
www.westphaliapress.org

# Braxton's Practical Cook Book

# Also from Westphalia Press
# westphaliapress.org

# BRAXTON'S

## PRACTICAL

# COOK BOOK.

---

COMPILED BY

## G. F. BRAXTON

CHEF OF WELLESLEY COLLEGE DURING THE PAST THREE
YEARS.

---

1886.

—

WALKER, YOUNG & CO., Book and Job Printers,
43 Kilby Street, Boston.

# TO THE PUBLIC.

---

Having had a practical experience as a cook in various hotels and institutions, and wishing to give the public a good, substantial cook book, both for family and hotel use, I have written this little volume for their benefit. These recipes have been studied as to economy, knowing full well that there are a good many cook books on the market that have been a failure in this respect. I do not wish to puff this book in the least, but will leave it to the candid judgment of those who will use it.

Hoping that I may add my mite to what is good and economical in cooking, I remain,

Truly yours,

GEORGE F. BRAXTON,
AUTHOR.

# CONTENTS.

# BRAXTON'S PRACTICAL COOK BOOK.

## HOW TO PREPARE STOCK FOR SOUPS.

The stock pot is the making of all good soups; that is to say if your kitchen is not provided with a stock pot it is impossible to make good soups. To prepare stock, take fresh beef bones, or bones of chicken, lamb, or any other fresh meat, crack them, put them into the pot, cover with cold water, set on the back of the stove and let it simmer all day, and if convenient, all night. The next morning strain, set in a cool place and when the grease rises, skim very carefully. Turn the stock, without any of the settlings, into the dish in which you wish to prepare the soup, and add the ingredients of whatever kind of soup you wish to prepare.

## FOR LIGHT SOUPS.

The stock for light soups, such as Macaroni, Barley, Rice, Sago and Tapioca, needs less boiling than for strong ones. Four hours is sufficient for light soups. For Consomme and all kinds of clarified soups the stock should be prepared the day before and the grease and settlings removed.

It should be clarified with the whites of eggs, usually the whites of four eggs to a quart of stock.

## ENGLISH MULLAGATAWNEY.

One gallon of good, clear stock, one chicken, six carrots, one onion, twelve potatoes. Cut the chicken in small, square pieces, the carrots lengthwise, mince the onion very fine, and add all to the stock; when nearly done add the potatoes, well sliced, and let them boil fifteen minutes. Season with salt and pepper to taste.

## FRENCH POTTAGE.

One gallon of stock, one quart of tomatoes, three carrots, two cups of vermicelli, one onion and one pound of ham. Boil the stock and after cooking the tomatoes, strain them, cut the carrots into dice, chop the onion, then cut the ham into squares and add the whole to the stock; when nearly done add the tomatoes, season to taste, and use a little cornstarch or flour for thickening.

## PRINCE ALBERT.

One and one-half gallons of stock, two cups of flake tapioca, two beef kidneys, one onion.  Parboil the kidneys in a separate dish, then cut it in squares, mince the onion and add both to the stock ; after the soup has boiled an hour, add the tapioca.  When done, season with salt and pepper, flavor with nutmeg or allspice, and thicken.  If not strong enough add Worcestershire Sauce.

## BEEF SOUP.

Four and one-half pounds of beef, one onion, two gallons of strong stock.  Let the stock boil then add the beef, cut into squares, and the onion minced fine.  When it boils remove all the scum that rises.  Season to taste and thicken, and add Halford Sauce or St. Clair wine.

## MUTTON BROTH.

The same as Beef Soup with the exception that two cups of rice are added.

## BEAN OR SPLIT PEA SOUP No. 1.

Soak one quart of beans over night, in the morning add sufficient water to cover them.  Let them boil and then rub through a collander and then through a fine sieve ; to this add one onion, a piece of veal or a knuckle of ham ; if necessary thicken.  Season to taste.  If not sufficiently light add two cups of boiling milk. Put some crumbs of bread, previously fried, in the tureen, pour over with the soup and send to the table.

## MRS. HASKIN'S BEAN OR PEA SOUP.

Made the same as No. 1, only the beans are not put through the collander or sieve.

## WELLESLEY COLLEGE.

Two and one-half gallons of good veal or chicken broth, one pound of liver. one dozen potatoes, one bunch of macaroni, one pound of butter and one onion.  Cut the liver into small pieces, mince the onion, break the macaroni into pieces about two inches in length, and add to the stock.  Remove all the scum that rises and add the butter and one teaspoonful of Curry powder.  When nearly done add the sliced potatoes ; season to taste.  Very nice.

## NOODLE SOUP.

One gallon of veal or chicken broth, boil thirty minutes. Make a paste of flour, eggs and perhaps a little baking powder; flour the paste and roll thin, then set in a cool, dry place to harden; then cut it into little strips and add to the soup and let it boil three minutes. Season with salt and pepper to taste. Flavor with nutmeg and thicken.

## MOCK TURTLE SOUP No. 1.

Two gallons of strong stock, a knuckle of veal or a calf's head, one onion, cloves and allspice tied in a bag; let the whole boil until done. Remove the bones and cut the meat into little pieces. Season with salt and pepper, and add a force meet egg and a force meet ball. Thicken. If too light add a teaspoonful of coloring, or two pieces of French paste. Slice two lemons into the tureen. This gives a rich color. After taking the soup from the stove, add not less than one cup of cooking wine.

## MOCK TURTLE SOUP No. 2.

Nearly the same as No. 1. Instead of using force meet eggs, use six hard boiled ones, cut into little squares. Slice two lemons into the tureen and add cooking wine to flavor it and it is ready to serve.

## GREEN TURTLE.

One turtle, remove the head and let it drain twelve hours. Dress it, being carefull not to break the eggs. When sufficiently cooked, remove all the fat. Cut the meat into small pieces, add the eggs, which have previously been boiled, also bouquet of sweet herbs to flavor. When done add one cup of cooking wine.

## CONSOMME.

One and one-half gallons of good strong stock, one onion; boil and put in the whites of six eggs to clarify it; season to taste and strain through a collander and then through a flannel bag, as for jellies; it should be very light. When done add one-half of a cup of brandy or cooking wine.

## VEGETABLE SOUP.

One gallon of clear stock, six carrots, two turnips, six potatoes and one onion. Chop the onion fine, cut the turnips and carrots into square pieces, add to the soup and boil. Fifteen minutes before it is done add the sliced potatoes. Use salt and pepper for seasoning.

## CHICKEN SOUP No. 1.

One chicken, one onion and one and one-half gallons of water. Chop the onion fine, cover the chicken with water, and when it is sufficiently cooked pick from the bones and cut in small pieces. Season to taste, flavor and thicken. I use nutmeg for flavoring.

## CHICKEN SOUP No. 2.

To be made the same as No. 1, with the exception that the bones are not taken out. The chicken is cut into square pieces and boiled. Flavor as in No. 1.

## BROWN SOUP.

One gallon of good strong stock, one onion minced and a little bag of fine herbs. Boil, season with salt and pepper to taste, and add a cup of cooking wine when it is done. Have ready some square pieces of bread fried brown, pour the soup over them and send to the table.

## SAGO OR TAPIOCA SOUP.

One gallon of chicken or veal broth and one cup of sago or tapioca. Put the sago to soak, boil the stock, and fifteen minutes before it is done add the sago. Season with salt and pepper and thicken if needed.

## OYSTER SOUP.

One quart of oysters and two gallons of chicken broth. After the broth is done add the oysters, season with salt and pepper to taste, a little butter and thicken. Very nice.

## CLAM SOUP.

One quart of clams, two gallons of water and one onion. Cut the clams, or chop them; mince the onion and boil all ten minutes. Add a piece of butter the size of a walnut, and season to taste. Liquor, if there is any with the clams, is a great improvement.

## LOBSTER SOUP.

One gallon of veal or chicken broth, the meat of six or eight large lobsters. Boil and add the lobsters, cut in small pieces, and let the whole simmer ten minutes and thicken. This is equal to any veal or chicken broth.

## RICE SOUP.

Two gallons of veal broth, or chicken, one onion and one and one-half cups of rice. Allow the rice to soak one hour, or more, and when the broth is done, add to it. Season and flavor as you wish, thicken and send to the table.

## VEAL BROTH.

One knuckle of veal, cover with water or stock, and boil till tender; pick the meat from the bones and cut in small pieces; add one cup of rice, cook and season to taste. Very nice for invalids.

## CLAM CHOWDER.

Two quarts of clams, one onion, twelve potatoes and three quarts of water. Mince the onion, cut the clams, and when the water has boiled put them with the water. When nearly done add the sliced potatoes, milk enough to give it a good color, season to taste. Split some crackers in the dish and pour the soup over them and it is ready to serve.

## OYSTER STEW.

One pint of oysters, water to cover. When they come to a boil, remove the scum, add butter the size of a walnut, a cup of hot milk, salt, pepper and serve.

## EGG SOUP.

One gallon of veal broth, season to taste with salt, pepper, a little spice, and just before it is ready to serve add six hard boiled eggs, cut in squares. Very nice.

## FOR CLARIFIED SOUPS.

Season and boil the stock, then clarify with the whites of eggs well beaten. Mix well together, boil five or seven minutes and strain through a flannel bag, as for jellies. Allow it to stand till the next day, heat and add the ingredients you wish.

## TOMATO SOUP.

One gallon of strong stock, one and one-half gallons of tomatoes; mix and add one small onion, mince fine, a bunch of fine herbs and boil slowly. Strain through a coarse sieve and then a fine strainer and boil again. Add pepper, salt and a cup of drawn butter, thicken a very little and if need be, add a little sugar. Pour this over fried bread crumbs and it is ready for the table.

### MOCK BISQUE.

One gallon of veal broth, season to taste, four eggs, flour enough to make a stiff paste, as for noodles, cut them out with a small round cutter, and bake. Add them to the soup allowing just time enough for them to soften and then serve.

### RABBIT SOUP.

One rabbit, cut into joints, cover with cold water, boil slowly till cooked ; strain, season to taste; cut the meat from the bones, and add to the liquor. Very nice for invalids.

### BEEF BROTH.

Beef broth or drippings from a roast of beef will make a very nice soup. Strain and season very lightly. Care should be taken to remove all the grease that rises. This will be nice for the sick.

### CORN SOUP.

One quart of chicken or veal broth, season to taste with salt and pepper. Add one can of corn, heat and serve.

### A QUICK TOMATO SOUP.

One pint of veal broth and one pint of tomatoes; boil, add a little butter, salt and pepper, thicken lightly and serve.

### CRACKER SOUP.

One pint of chicken broth, season to taste with salt, pepper and a walnut of butter, and thicken with cracker dust, and it will be found very nice for invalids.

### ITALIAN CONSOMME.

Strong stock, well clarified, season as for Mock Turtle, and just before serving add some Italian Paste.

## OYSTERS IN ALL STYLES.

### ESCALLOPED OYSTERS.

Put a layer of bread or cracker crumbs into your baking pan, next one of oysters, then one of butter, and sprinkle salt and pepper over each layer. Fill the dish in this way, then moisten the top with milk or water and bake in a moderate oven.

## FANCY ROAST.

One pint of oysters stewed in the liquor; add salt, pepper and butter the size of a walnut. Pour this over toasted bread, garnish with parsley and serve.

## PLAIN ROAST.

One pint of oysters cooked in the liquor, with salt, pepper and butter added. Serve in a deep dish garnished with parsley.

## BROILED OYSTERS.

Wipe six large oysters dry, sprinkle cracker crumbs over them, lay them on a gridiron and broil till brown. Lay them in a plate and pour melted butter over them.

## OYSTERS ON THE HALF SHELL.

Open as many oysters as you need and leave them on one-half of the shell. Serve in a dish with a piece of lemon, salt and pepper. Use vinegar if preferred.

## BROILED OYSTERS.

Put six large oysters, in the shell, on the coals, and let them remain until they open; then remove the top shell, pour melted butter over them and serve on a napkin.

## BOXED OR CREAMED OYSTERS.

One pint of oysters and one quart of sweet cream or milk; boil the milk, and while boiling, add the oysters and season to taste; thicken with flour or cornstarch. Have some round, well baked loaves of bread ready, remove the top and all the crumbs; then take the box or crust of bread, put some hot fat into it and fry it brown; place the oysters in this and serve in a platter.

## PICKLED OYSTERS.

Place some large oysters in a jar; scald sufficient vinegar to cover them, allow it to cool, then pour it over them with whole cloves and allspice added. Set in a cool place for two or three days before using.

## OYSTER PATTIES.

Stew a quart of oysters in a little water and milk enough to give a good color, season to taste and thicken as for a stew, have some nice puff paste, cut in pattie shape, and bake quickly. When done make a hole in the centre of each, fill with oysters and serve on a platter. Very nice.

## BAKED OYSTER PIE.

Stew one quart of oysters in the liquor and sufficient water to cover them, with a little salt, pepper and butter added; thicken, put into the dish and cover with a nice puff paste and bake in a quick oven.

## OYSTER POTPIE.

This may be made the same as baked oyster pie and serve nice dumplings with it.

## OYSTER SALAD.

One quart of oysters, or as many as you will need; cut in halves, season with salt, pepper and sweet oil to improve it; cut some hard boiled eggs in squares and mix with the oysters; cut some fresh lettuce heads fine, put a layer of lettuce, then one of oysters, and so on. Have the last layer of lettuce and cover with Mayonaise Dressing.

## DRESSING FOR THE ABOVE.

Six hard boiled eggs; remove the whites, rub the yolks through a fine sieve, add one-half teaspoonful of mustard, a little salt and cayenne pepper; add the yolk of an egg and a little sweet oil from time to time, till you have enough; you should use a wooden spoon in making it and make it in a cool place; add a little vinegar, as much as you think you will need, but keep it stiff so that it will remain on the top of the salad; if you find it to be hard add the juice of one lemon. Keep on ice till you wish to serve.

## BOILED OYSTERS (In shell.)

Wash six large oysters and put them one by one into boiling water and let them remain five minutes; remove, wipe dry, squeeze the juice of one lemon over them and send to the table; have some melted butter ready to pour over then. They will be found to be delicious indeed.

## DEVILED OYSTERS.

One quart of oysters, one cup of cracker dust, two eggs, the juice of one lemon and some melted butter; wipe the oysters, lay on a flat dish, beat the eggs well, add the pepper, cayenne, and lemon juice and pour this mixture over the oysters; have ready some hot butter and lard mixed, take the oysters from the mixture and dip in the cracker dust and fry brown. Serve with German Mustard.

## FRICASSEED OYSTERS.

One pint of good veal or chicken broth, one ounce of ham or salt pork, one onion minced fine; boil all together with a little pepper, salt and butter; thicken and set on the back of the stove; then add the oysters and a little chopped parsley. The oysters will cook on the back of the stove.

## OYSTERS IN BATTER.

One pint of oysters; mix one egg, one pint of flour and perhaps a little baking powder, into a smooth paste, dip the oysters into it one by one, and fry in hot fat.

## OYSTER PATES.

One quart of oysters cut fine with a knife, not a chopping knife, one spoonful of butter drawn in one cup of milk, thicken with cornstarch or flour; season to taste; drain the liquor from the oysters and stir them into the mixture. Have ready some puff paste, baked brown, fill with the oysters, set in the oven for a few moments, serve at once.

## CREAMED OYSTER PIE.

Line a pie plate with puff paste; butter some stale bread and put in the bottom, then put on the top crust and bake quickly. When done, carefully lift the top crust, fill with creamed oysters, replace the top crust and heat five minutes. This makes a very good side dish.

# LOBSTERS.

## CURRIED LOBSTER.

Cut the meat of six large lobsters into small pieces, boil the veal or chicken broth, season to taste; add one-half teaspoonful of Curry powder; the powder should be dissolved in cold water, that it may be smooth; thicken as for any stew; set on the back of the stove, add the lobster allow it to heat, then serve.

## DEVILED LOBSTER.

Meat of six lobsters, half teaspoonful of mustard, one gallon veal or chicken broth. Boil the stock, add the mixed mustard, season to taste and if necessary add one teaspoonful of vinegar; thicken and serve on toast.

## LOBSTER IN BATTER.

The meat of six lobsters cut in strips; mix a smooth batter with a little baking powder, dip the lobster in it and fry in hot fat. Drain in a collander and serve on napkins. Excellent.

## SMOTHERED LOBSTER.

The meat of six large lobsters cut in squares; place in a dripping pan, cover with gravy from fricasseed chicken or veal, allow it to set in the oven ten minutes; when done add some sprigs of parsley and serve with toast.

## LOBSTER IN CRUMBS.

Cut the meat of three lobsters and salt them; beat three eggs well, dip the lobster in it, roll in crumbs and fry a golden brown. Serve with Tomato sauce.

## FRICASSEED LOBSTER.

The meat of six lobsters and chicken broth; cut the lobster, cook as for fricasseed chicken, add a little butter, flavor with nutmeg, season to taste, thicken, and if not sufficiently light add one cup of hot milk; serve on toast.

## STEWED LOBSTER.

Meat of six large lobsters, veal broth and one minced onion; boil, and add the lobster cut in strips, season to taste, flavor with nutmeg, thicken and serve.

## LOBSTER CROQUETTES.

Mince the meat of six lobsters, three or four eggs well beaten and bread crumbs softened in milk or hot water. Mix, flavor with nutmeg, season to taste. Have it very stiff, mould into rolls, dip in beaten egg, roll in flour and fry brown, and serve with lobster sauce; garnish with parsley.

## LOBSTER CUTLETS.

Made the same as the above. Wash the shell, fill with the mixture and serve.

## LOBSTER SALAD. No. 1.

The meat of six lobsters cut in squares, seasoned to taste with salt, pepper and vinegar. Mix with this, six hard boiled eggs cut in pieces; cut three heads of lettuce and have a layer of lettuce, one of lobster and so on. Cover with mayonaise dressing and serve.

## LOBSTER SALAD. No. 2.

Made the same as No. 1, only the lettuce is cut fine and mixed with the lobster. Serve with mayonaise dressing.

## LOBSTER PUDDING.

Boil three lobsters, remove the meat and pound in a mortar, four eggs well beaten, one pint of milk, mix as for custard, season to taste and flavor with cinnamon; also add a little Worcestershire or Halford Sauce, the lobster and a cup of bread or cracker crumbs. Line the dish with ham or salt pork, pour in the pudding, cook, and serve with Anchovy sauce.

## ESCALLOPED LOBSTERS. No. 1.

Made the same as escalloped oysters, with a little Anchovy added and bake.

## ESCALLOPED LOBSTERS. No. 2.

The meat of six lobsters, cut fine and mixed with four well beaten eggs, some bread crumbs, a little cream and Anchovy sauce. Season to taste and add a walnut of butter. Mix well, fill the shell, bake in a quick oven and send to the table in the shell. Very nice.

## CRABS.

Crabs may be used in the same way as lobsters, but it requires a longer time to cook them. Crabs may be boiled, fricasseed, stewed, deviled, curried, fried in crumbs, in batter, escalloped or broiled.

## FRIED TURTLE STEAK.

Cut the steak from the thickest part of the turtle, as thin as possible, season to taste and fry brown. Serve with mushroom sauce. A very wholesome dish.

## FRICASSEED TURTLE.

Two pounds of turtle cut in squares; boil some chicken or veal broth and one minced onion. When done add a can of mushrooms, season to taste, sprinkle on a little parsley, flavor with allspice, thicken and serve on toast. Garnish with red beets and add the juice of one lemon and serve.

## FRIED CLAMS.

Drain the liquor from one quart of clams, drop into hot fat, and they are ready to serve when they are browned.

## CLAMS IN BATTER.

A quart of clams cut fine. Make a paste with a little baking powder added, dip the clams in this, fry brown and serve.

## CURRIED CLAMS.

Drain one quart of clams. Boil some chicken or veal broth, one onion, season to taste, flavor with curry powder and add the clams ; cook, thicken and after adding a little butter it will be ready to serve.

## DEVILED CLAMS.

One quart of clams cut, not chopped ; chicken or veal broth, one half teaspoonful of mustard ; season to taste, thicken, add clams and butter, cook and then serve.

## ESCALLOPED CLAMS.

The same as escalloped oysters. Very nice.

## BAKED CLAM PIE.

Halve a quart of clams, not chop them ; boil some veal or chicken broth, one onion, then put in the clams; season to taste, butter, flavor with nutmeg, thicken as for any pie, make a nice crust, cover and bake.

## CLAM CHOWDER.

Two quarts of clams, one dozen potatoes cut in squares, one minced onion, four quarts of water. Let the water boil, then add the onion, potatoes and the clams, cut in small pieces ; season to taste, add butter and salt pork, and when done add three pints of milk and send to the table.

# FISH.

## BROILED FISH.

To boil fish, either salt or fresh, a bright fire is needed. Sprinkle a little flour or Indian meal over it, and after being broiled pour drawn butter over it, garnish with parsley and send to the table.

## BOILED CODFISH.

One codfish; boil in a fish kettle with water to cover; season to taste and serve with butter or cream sauce.

## BOILED SALMON.

Boil as for any fish, add a cup of vinegar to make it hold together and serve.

## SHIRRED PICKEREL.

Dress the pickerel and boil with sufficient water to cover, with one minced onion; season to taste, flavor with nutmeg and add to this one cup of cream and three-quarters of a pound of pork. Thicken, and when ready to serve add some nice sprigs of parsley.

## BAKED STUFFED BLUEFISH.

Wash, wipe and dress as you would any fish; cut into dice with a sharp knife, and bake; add some salt pork, season to taste and serve with brown sauce.

## BAKED SHAD.

The same as bluefish. To smother shad, add one minced onion, cover with parsley, a little salt pork, season and bake.

## TO CORN FISH.

Salt the fish as you would corned beef, according to the number of pounds, and it is ready any time when you wish to use it. Very convenient to have in case you should be short of fresh fish or meats.

To boil or bake any kind of fish, you should be governed by the foregoing recipes. As there are so many ways of frying fish, it is not necessary to mention them.

# EGGS.

Eggs are very nutritious and may be prepared in a variety of ways to suit almost any taste.

## SHIRRED EGGS.

Break two eggs into a dish, sprinkle with pepper and salt, place in the oven and when the whites set, serve.

## POACHED EGGS. No. 1.

Break two eggs into a basin of hot water, allow the whites to set, remove with an egg skimmer and serve.

## POACHED EGGS. No. 2.

Break two eggs, add a teaspoonful of milk, beat well and cook in the frying pan. Serve in an oval dish.

## POACHED EGGS. No. 3.

Add one-half a cup of vinegar to some water and drop two eggs into it; after the whites have set serve on cream toast and lay some sprigs of parsley around the dish.

## SCRAMBLED EGGS.

Two well beaten eggs, cooked in a frying pan, stir all the time while cooking. Excellent.

## OMELETTE.

Beat two eggs with a little milk, cook in a spider, roll and serve in a hot platter. Cheese or other kinds may be made by mixing the cheese with the milk and eggs.

## OMELETTE SOUFFLÉ.

Beat the yolks separately and cook ; then beat the whites to a stiff froth, cover the omelette, place in the oven to brown lightly ; then sprinkle powdered sugar over it and put a little cooking spirits around the dish, light, and send to the table.

## EGG CUTLET.

Cut two hard boiled eggs in slices, dip into a beaten egg, then in crumbs. Drop into hot fat, fry brown and serve with drawn butter.

## DROPPED EGGS ON TOAST.

Drop two broken eggs into boiling water, let the whites set and serve on buttered toast.

## EGGS.—Sur la Platee.

Six eggs, one tablespoonful of butter or nice drippings, pepper and salt to taste. Melt the butter, break the eggs carefully, into this dust with pepper and salt and set in a moderate oven till the whites are done and serve in the same dish in which they were baked.

## TOAST EGGS.

Cover the bottom of a dish with rounds of delicate toast or what is better, rounds of stale bread dipped in beaten egg and fried quickly in butter or nice drippings; place the dish immediately in front of a glowing fire and toast over them as many pieces of corned pork or ham as there are eggs; hold the meat so that it will toast quickly and so that the drippings may fall upon the eggs; turn the eggs around so that they may cook evenly; when a crust forms they are done. Do not send the meat to the table, but pepper the eggs a little, remove with the egg turner, taking care not to break them.

## BAKED EGGS. No. 1.

Six eggs, four tablespoonfuls of good veal, beef or poultry gravy, the latter preferred, one handful of bread crumbs, six rounds of fried or toasted bread; put the gravy, bread and eggs into a shallow baking dish, add pepper, salt and sprinkle the crumbs over them and bake five minutes in a quick oven; remove the eggs carefully and place upon the toasted bread, which has previously been put in a hot platter; add a little cream and if you like, some chopped parsley and onion to the gravy left in the pan, boil and pour over it.

## BAKED EGGS. No. 2.

Six eggs, one cup of good gravy, chicken is best, one teaspoonful of chopped parsley, one onion chopped fine and one handful of crumbs, bread or cracker, pepper and salt to taste; put enough gravy into a baking dish to cover the bottom, set in the oven and when it bubbles put in the eggs, do not crowd them, and let them bake three minutes. While these are cooking, add to the other gravy the parsley and onion, heat it; a little pepper and salt and some crumbs should be sprinkled over the eggs before they are put in the oven. When the eggs have been in the oven three minutes pour the rest of the gravy over them, more pepper, salt and crumbs and then allow the whites to set and send to the table in the dish in which they are baked. A very savory dish.

## FRICASSEED EGGS.

Pour some nice gravy over six hard boiled eggs cut in pieces, then pour this over some toasted bread, send to the table, garnish with parsley.

## EGG CUTLET.

Six hard boiled eggs, sliced, dipped in a beaten egg, and fried in hot lard.

### ESCALLOPED EGGS. Raw.

Six eggs, four or five tablespoons of ground or minced ham, a little chopped parsley, very little minced onion, two tablespoonfuls of cream and a little melted butter, salt and pepper to taste, one-half of a cup of bread crumbs, moistened with milk and a spoonful of melted butter; line the bottom of a small, deep dish, well buttered, with the soaked bread crumbs, add a layer of chopped ham, parsley and onion. Set in the oven, closely covered, until smoking hot. Meanwhile beat the eggs to a stiff froth, season with pepper and salt, add the cream and melted butter, pour over the ham, cover and set in the oven and allow the whites to set.

### ESCALLOPED EGGS. Hard Boiled.

Six hard boiled eggs cut in thin slices, one cup of bread crumbs moistened with a little good gravy, a little milk or cream, one-half of a cup of drawn butter into which has been beaten the yolk of one egg, one cup of minced ham, tongue, poultry, cold halibut, salmon or cod, pepper and salt to taste; put a layer of crumbs in the bottom of a buttered baking dish, then a layer of sliced egg which has been dipped in the butter, then a layer of minced meat and so on, until the egg is used; place in the oven, bake and serve.

### POACHED EGGS.

Six eggs, one teaspoonful of vinegar, one pint of boiling water; add the vinegar to the water, dip some slices of bread into a beaten egg with a little parsley added, then fry brown; put the eggs into the hot vinegar and water, cook, place them on the toast and serve. Very nice.

# ROAST MEATS.

In order to be able to roast different kinds of meats, one must be able to regulate the oven correctly, and of course, the oven should be just right; not too hot, or the meat will roast too fast or burn, then again, you must be sure that it is sufficiently heated. A little experience is all that is necessary. One should learn to give the meat just time enough to cook thoroughly, and send immediately to the table.

### ROAST BEEF.

Place the rib to be roasted into a dripping pan, season to taste, dust a little flour over it, put in the oven; baste with a little stock or dish gravy, turn and when sufficiently cooked remove from the oven and send to the table together with the gravy made from where the meat has roasted.

## ROAST LAMB.

Crack the joints of a rib or leg of lamb, season with salt, dust a little flour over it, place in a pan and cook; remove and serve with mint sauce.

## ROAST VEAL.

Remove the bone from a leg of veal, stuff with some firm bread dressing, tie the ends to prevent the dressing from running out, cook and serve with brown sauce.

## ROAST PORK.

Joint a rib of pork, salt and sprinkle a little flour over it, roast and carve, serve with apple sauce.

## ROAST HAM.

Boil a nice sugar cured ham, then brown and serve with champagne sauce.

## ROAST TURKEY.

Dress a turkey, stuff it with a nice dressing, tie the neck and sew the gash to prevent the dressing from coming out, place in a dripping pan and roast. Serve with cranberry sauce.

## ROAST CHICKEN.

Dress the chicken nicely, removing the first joint; stuff with a nice dressing, tie the wings and legs so that it will lay nicely in the pan; sprinkle with salt and pour a little water over it that it may not burn; after browning, baste with the gravy that is in the pan, turn, that it may cook evenly, then send it to the table when done, with the gravy made from the drippings in the pan.

## ROAST GOOSE.

Dress, wash and wipe dry and if very strong, soak over night in salt and water to cleanse it. When ready to use, make a nice dressing of bread, potatoes and one chopped onion, with a little sage to flavor, season with salt and pepper. Fill the goose with the dressing and roast. Chop the giblets and make a sauce for it. Serve with jelly or apple sauce.

## ROAST DUCK.

The same as for goose, and serve with jelly.

In roasting game of any kind, the preceding recipes should be followed.

## ROAST BEEF.

Soak over night a piece of salt, rump beef, to remove all the sharp taste of salt, roast till done and serve with weed salad.

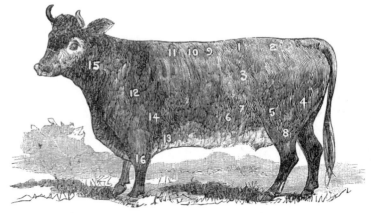

| HIND QUARTER. | FORE QUARTER. |
|---|---|
| 1  Sirloin. | 9   Fore Rib—five ribs. |
| 2  Rump. | 10  Middle Rib—four ribs. |
| 3  Edgebone. | 11  Chuck—three ribs. |
| 4  Buttock. | 12  Shoulder. |
| 5  Veiny Piece. | 13  Brisket. |
| 6  Thick Flank. | 14  Clod. |
| 7  Thin Flank, | 15  Neck or Sticking Piece. |
| 8  Leg. | 16  Shin. |
|  | 17  Chuck. |

| | |
|---|---|
| 1  Leg. | 4  Neck—best end. |
| 2  Loin—best end. | 5  Neck—scrag end. |
| 3  Loin—chump end. | 6  Shoulder. |
|  | 7  Breast. |

1 Shoulder.  
2 Neck.  
3 Haunch.

4 Breast.  
5 Scrag.

1 Leg.  
2 Hind Loin.  
3 Fore Loin.  
4 Spare Rib.  
5 Ham.  
6 Belly or Spring.

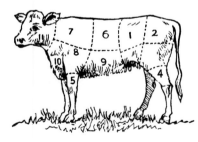

1 Loin—best end.  
2 Loin—chump end.  
3 Fillet.  
4 Hind Knuckle.  
5 Fore Knuckle.

6 Neck—best end.  
7 Scrag End.  
8 Blade Bone.  
9 Breast—best end.  
10 Breast—brisket end.

## BOILED MUTTON.

Boil a leg of mutton till most done, add one cup of vinegar to keep it firm, and when done serve with caper or piquant sauce.

## BOILED HAM.

Boil till done and serve either hot or cold.

## BOILED CORNED BEEF.

Wash and boil a piece of corned beef till tender, and serve with vegetables as a regular boiled dinner.

## BEEF TONGUES.

Boil a salt or fresh tongue, and when tender, pour cold water over it and peel it; the cold water makes it peel more easily. Slice nicely and serve.

## TURKEY.

Boil till tender and serve with oyster sauce.

## CHICKEN.

Boil till tender and serve with salt pork or with butter sauce.

## SAUSAGE. A la Duchesse.

Put the sausage into boiling water and boil till done; this makes a very nice dish for breakfast or luncheon.

## BOILED PIGS' FEET.

Prepare the feet and boil them; when done allow them to cool, souse in vinegar and they will be nice for a luncheon.

## BOILED PIGS' JOLES.

Boil the head of a pig and when sufficiently cooked serve with butter sauce; or, chop fine, flavor and season with pepper and salt and make into a cheese. Hogs-head cheese is excellent.

# BROILED MEATS.

Broiling, as well as roasting, must be thoroughly understood to be well done. Experience will teach one very much, as to which kind of meat require quick broiling, and which do not.

## BEEFSTEAK.

For broiling beefsteak, a bright charcoal fire is excellent; season the steak to taste with salt, or salt and pepper, cook it as you prefer it, either rare or well done. Just before serving, add butter and garnish with parsley.

## BROILED HAM.

A medium fire is required for broiling ham or bacon, as bacon is sometimes very fat and the drippings from it will brighten the fire, and you must be careful not to burn it.

## BROILED LIVER.

Slice the liver, broil and pour butter over it and serve with salt pork or bacon.

## BROILED PIGS' FEET.

Broil some cold boiled feet nicely, pour butter over them and send to the table.

## BROILED CHICKEN.

One chicken; split it from the back, flatten the joints so that it may lay on the griddle nicely, season with salt and put over a bright fire; then place in the oven until thoroughly cooked, pour butter over it to make a nice gravy and serve.

## BROILED VEAL CUTLET.

Have the cutlet steak of medium thickness, broil, season with salt, pour butter over it and serve.

## BROILED SALT PORK.

Cut the pork in thin slices, broil over a medium fire, serve with eggs or liver.

## LAMB CHOPS.

Place some nice chops on a broiler and broil over a slow fire after seasoning; pour melted butter over it and serve.

## BROILED TRIPE.

Use honeycomb tripe, broil over a quick fire, pour over melted butter, garnish with parsley and serve.

## PARTRIDGE OR SNIPE.

Broil over a quick fire, season, pour over a little melted butter and serve on toast.

# ENTREES.

It is quite an accomplishment for a cook to be able to use the remnants of a meal and make a delicate and palatable dish, yet it can be done. Such economy is a great help, and should be practiced by all. Economy in little things makes a great difference in the grocery bill. The author, Mr. Braxton, has always been employed by economical people and therefore calls your attention to this.

## BEEFSTEAK PIE.

Cut the pieces of steak, left from the table, into little squares, stew them in water or clear stock; season with salt, pepper, a little butter, thicken as for any stew, and put in the dish; make a nice crust, cover and bake to a golden brown and serve.

## LAMB PIE.

Use the remnants of lamb that cannot be used for anything else, stew as you would beef steak, add to it one onion minced fine, season to taste, add one tablespoonful of butter, thicken, put in a baking dish, cover with a nice crust and bake.

## HAMBURG BEEFSTEAK.

One and one-half pounds of minced beef, one onion, minced; remove all the sinews from the meat; season with salt and pepper, make into cakes; place them in a pan, pour butter over them to keep them moist and bake; make a nice gravy with what is left in the pan and serve.

## BLANQUETTE DE VEAU.

One and one-half pounds of veal cut in squares, one onion, minced; put in a sauce pan, cover with water and boil till done; season with salt, pepper and a tablespoonful of butter, also the juice of one lemon, some chopped parsley, one-half a cup of wine and Worcestershire sauce or tomato ketchup; thicken and serve.

## RICE CROQUETTES.

Soak three cups of rice over night; the next morning boil and add three eggs; after it is done sweeten to taste, flavor with lemon or vanilla; after it cools, add three or four tablespoons of flour so it will hold together, and make into balls or strips; dip these in beaten egg, then in flour and fry in drippings. Serve on napkins.

## VEAL OR POULTRY CROQUETTES.

Mix one pound of minced veal, two cups of cooked rice, one raw egg; season to taste, flavor; make into shape as for rice croquettes and make a sauce of veal or chicken and serve with them.

## HAM CROQUETTES.

Made the same as the above, only add to it a little chopped parsley and it will be very satisfactory. Serve with champagne sauce.

## CHAMPAGNE SAUCE.

One pint of water, a piece of butter the size of an egg, let it come to a boil, thicken with cornstarch, a little salt, sufficient coloring to make it a light brown; remove from the fire when the cornstarch has cooked, color and add some hard cider, or champagne cider; the latter is best if it can be procured.

## BEEF A LA MODE.

Two and one-half pounds of beef, rump, trimmed nicely; some carrots, cut in thin lengthwise pieces; then with a larding needle, lard the carrots through and through, as thick as you can; prepare some pork, a firm piece, in the same manner as the carrots. Put the beef in a sauce pan, cover with water and one-third vinegar, add to it one minced onion, cloves, pepper, allspice and salt and let it remain until the next day, and cook; remove the beef when done and thicken the liquor, add to it some Worcestershire sauce, strain and serve with the beef. Carve crosswise so that the carrots may be seen. Serve with gravy and garnish with parsley.

## FRICASSEED CHICKEN.

Clean and cut in joints one nice chicken, place in a sauce pan, cover with water and boil; remove all the scum that rises; add one minced onion, season to taste, flavor with nutmeg, thicken with flour or cornstarch and when done add one cup of boiling milk and some butter, about one tablespoonful; then serve.

## FRICASSEED CHICKEN. A L'Americain.

Made the same as the above except that no milk is used. Sprinkle chopped parsley over it and serve.

## BROWN FRICASSEED CHICKEN.

The same as the above only color with burnt sugar or flour.

## FRICASSEED CHICKEN. A la Chevaliere.

The same as the preceding. Make some nice puff paste, cut in diamonds, bake and serve on the fricassee.

## STEWED CHICKEN.

Dress and cut in squares, one chicken, cover with water and cook. Add one minced onion, season with salt and pepper, one tablespoonful of butter, thicken and add a little chopped parsley.

## CHICKEN STEW WITH DUMPLINGS.

Prepare a plain stew, and some flour dumplings to serve with it.

## CHICKEN PIE.

Prepare the same as for a stew, only you should have it thicker than for a stew. Pour it into a baking dish, cover with a nice crust and bake a golden brown.

## CHICKEN POT-PIE.

Make the same as the above and steam, instead of baking it.

## CHICKEN HASH.

Cut some cold chicken or turkey very fine, and as many hard boiled eggs as you think you will need, also cut fine; mix these with a little moisture of some kind, pepper and salt to taste. Have it just warm and serve on toast.

## MINCED CHICKEN.

Chop some cold chicken, season, add a little wetting, Put in a sauce pan, heat, then make a hole in the centre and put in a dropped egg and serve.

## PINIONS OF FOWLS.

Clean the first joints of a chicken's wings, remove all the pin feathers and stew; add one minced onion, season to taste, thicken; remove from the fire and add one pint of nice oysters, let it set three minutes and serve.

## SMOTHERED CHICKEN.

Dress and split one chicken as for broiling, just cover with water and boil till done. Remove the chicken and add to the broth, one pint of oysters, some cloves and chopped parsley, season to taste, thicken and serve on toast.

## POTTED CHICKEN.

If you have some cold chicken remove the meat from the bones, or, if you prefer, stew a chicken cut in squares, and when done, season and add one cup of cooked rice; mix nicely and serve.

## GIBLET STEW.

Cut the giblets, stew with a little water, season and it will make a nice side dish.

## CHICKEN LIVERS.  A la Brochette.

Wash, wipe and cut in two pieces the livers; cut slices of bacon about the same size, broil them and when done pour a sauce of melted butter, lemon juice and pepper over it. Serve hot.

## BRAISED DUCK.

Prepare the chicken or duck as for roasting. Line the bottom of a pan with strips of salt pork or bacon, put the duck in next sprinkle spices and onion juice over it, baste frequently; when done remove the duck, thicken and strain the gravy and serve.

## BRAISED STUFFED MUTTON.

Dress a leg of mutton as you would a leg of veal for roasting; place in a pan, sprinkle with salt and pepper add some whole cloves and allspice and put a little water in the pan; roast and baste frequently. When done, remove and make a nice gravy with what is left in the pan, add some salt pork and chopped onion. Then strain and serve with the mutton.

## BRAISED BEEF.

The same as mutton, except that Worcestershire sauce is added.

## RAGOUT OF BEEF.

Cut some cold roast beef into squares, stew it with a little water, one onion, minced, one or two carrots to give it a vegetable flavor. Cook and add some Halford sauce or tomato ketchup; season to taste, thicken, remove the carrots and send to the table around the meat.

## HARICOT MUTTON.

Cut two pounds of mutton in squares, wash and stew with a little water, one minced onion, two carrots and six potatoes cut crosswise; stew slowly and remove before the vegetables break. Add some Halford or Worcestershire sauce. Thicken, season to taste and serve.

## IRISH STEW.

Cut the cold lamb and beefsteak that was left from breakfast, in small pieces. Wash, cover with water and stew with one chopped onion and six potatoes. Season to taste, thicken and serve.

## QUEEN FRITTERS.

One pint of water, six eggs and two ounces of leaf lard. Have the water boiling and add sufficient flour to make a smooth and quite stiff dough, then stir in the lard. Fry in nice drippings by spoonfuls. They will be hollow and should be served with sweet sauce.

## CORN FRITTERS.

One can of corn and one and one half pints of flour. Mix the flour with milk and add to the corn, also mix three raw eggs with it and a little baking powder to spring it. Add a little sugar and fry nicely and serve with lemon sauce.

## SPANISH PUFFS.

Two eggs and one and one-half pints of flour; mix the flour to a smooth paste with milk, add to it the eggs, one-third of a cup of sugar also some nutmeg, cinnamon and allspice, not enough, however, to make it very dark. Mix well together, add a little baking powder and fry the same as corn fritters. Dust powdered sugar over them and serve.

## CREAM FRITTERS.

One pint of milk and two cups of sugar; boil the milk and thicken with cornstarch; flavor with lemon or vanilla, pour into a flat, square dish, allow it to cool, then cut into squares, dip in egg, then in cracker crumbs and fry brown. To be served with apple jelly or wine sauce.

## BLUEBERRY FRITTERS.

Blueberry or raspberry fritters may be made the same as corn fritters. Very nice. Serve with sweet sauce.

# CORNED MEATS.

It is very necessary to be able to corn and also to pickle. If you should have more meat or fish on hand than you could possibly use for a few days, it would be absolutely necessary to be able to take care of them, as no economical housekeeper or steward would wish to lose it. Great care should be taken to save all the little things, as they count a good deal in the course of a year.

## TO CORN BEEF.

For twenty-five pounds of beef, use six quarts of water, two pounds of coarse salt, one-half teaspoonful of saltpetre, one-half pound of brown sugar or one pint of molasses. Mix all the ingredients with the water, boil, remove the scum as it rises; take from the fire and when cool pour over the beef, which has previously been put into a firkin. This will preserve beef the year round. Increase or decrease the quantity as you wish.

To pickle pork or beef for a short time, place the meat in a barrel. First a layer of salt then one of beef, and so on till the meat is used. Cover closely and let it stand four or five days; then remove the scum that has risen, if there be any, and pour cold water over it, enough to cover it. If kept in a cool place, meat will, in this way, be good for three or four weeks.

In corning meats care should be taken to soak the meat in water a while, otherwise the blood will rise and sour, and that will spoil all the meat.

Let it soak twenty-four hours before pickling, this will prevent it souring so quickly.

Fresh meat will not keep good in the larder with milk, butter and other liquids or hot food. Some people have an idea that all of their milk and butter can be kept in the larder together with fresh meat. But the dampness from the milk will make the meat mould, and the strength from the meat will cause the milk to sour. In order to keep meat properly, one should use a cold blast refrigerator, having hooks on which to hang the meat. It should have a door in the top or side to put in the ice, and should be lined with zinc. It will keep for a long time in this way. For milk, a one story dairy, built in the ground is best, or a patent Vermont house dairy; provide shelves for the milk, around the room and quite near the ground and in this way it will keep nicely. One would naturally think it would be expensive to have both of these, but you would very soon make it pay for itself in the amount it would save. Also butter should be kept in a dry place, otherwise it will grow strong in a short time.

### PICKLED PIGS' FEET.

Boil the feet, allow them to cool, place in a keg, cover with scalded vinegar and water, add some whole cloves and spices. Have the keg air-tight until ready for use.

### TO SOUSE TRIPE, ETC.

Boil four quarts of water and vinegar, two-thirds water and one-third vinegar; remove all the scum as it rises ; after it has boiled allow it to cool then place the tripe, pig's ears or lamb's tongues in the keg and pour the vinegar and water over them. Also put in about one tablespoonful of cloves and three blades of mace and fasten air-tight. This may be eaten cold or fried in batter or in crumbs for a side dish.

### CORNED FISH.

Split in the centre, and if the back bone is very large it should be removed. Sprinkle the bottom of the keg with rock salt, then a layer of fish and another layer of salt and so on, the fish should be placed with the skin down; the last layer should be of salt and thicker than the others. Keep in a dry, cool place and it will be ready for use in three or five days. When any is wanted for use it should be allowed to soak over night in cold water and it will be ready to cook for a meal. After the fish are carefully put into the keg cover with cold water.

### CORNED MACKEREL.

The same as the above, fasten air-tight, keep for winter use and either boil or broil.

### CORNED ALEVIVES.

These are so small that it would be useless to split. Otherwise prepare the same as mackerel.

## SMOKED SALMON.

To smoke salmon or halibut, prepare the pickle as for corning beef, and allow it to cool. Split the fish in the back and lay it skin down, in a dish; pour the pickle over it and let it stand three weeks. Then remove the fish, rub salt lightly over it and let it drain well; hang it up in a dry, warm room, on a beam, build a hard wood fire under it, a corn-cob one would be better, and let it smoke, not blaze, for three days. As some do not like it raw, it may be cooked in the following way:—cut in slices, pour boiling water over it to take the salt taste out, then frizzle with butter or broil. Be sure to pour the water over it before undertaking to frizzle it.

## TO CAN FRESH SALMON.

Boil the salmon until just done, season to taste, place in a deep tin dish about the size of the dish in which you are going to can it, and cover, then press well; place in the can, be sure that it is air tight; serve cold or make salads.

## PICKLED SALMON.

Boil the salmon till done and pick out the bones; boil some vinegar and water, two-thirds water and one-third vinegar, and some whole cloves; let it cool and pour over the salmon. Have the keg air-tight and you should use your judgment as to the quantity of vinegar and water to use, enough to a little more than cover it.

## CANNED LOBSTER.

Boil the lobster fifteen minutes, and remove all the meat from the shell, remove the little dark string in the back, season with salt, place in a can with its own liquid and fasten air-tight. Use cold or make into salads.

## PICKLED LOBSTER.

Prepare the pickle the same as for salmon, let it cool and pour over the lobster, let it stand five or ten days before using.

## PICKLED OYSTERS.

Drain all the liquor from a quart of nice oysters; make a pickle of scalded water and vinegar, cool and pour over the oysters; add a half dozen cloves and one blade of mace; let them stand one week before using.

## PICKLED CLAMS.

The same as oysters, only pour the vinegar over them hot.

## CANNED CLAMS.

Scald the clams in their own liquor, place in a can or jar, seal tightly and have on hand to fry or for a chowder.

# MISCELLANEOUS DISHES.

It is necessary that one should know something about the scrap bag or miscellaneous dishes, that is, they must know what to do with the little pieces of meat or bread, in order to be a good housekeeper. Never waste anything, no matter how little it may be, if it will do anyone any good it should always be saved. Take care of the pennies and the dollars will take care of themselves. A wealthy person should know how to take care of his or her property, or they will lose it, and by saving a poor person may become rich. As the proverb says: "It is a hard road to success and an easy road to the door of poverty." When we waste little things we are surely throwing away money, only in very small amounts of course. The time may come when you would be thankful for something you had wasted in years that are past. And it will seem as if all friends had deserted you, when you apply to them for help. They will wonder, and perhaps say: "Where is that hundred dollars that you had such a short time ago?" They cannot see what could have become of it in such a short time ; and if you should ask for the loan of a little they would not care to let you have it, as they would naturally think that you could not take proper care of any amount, however small it might be. So we must try and save everything that may be of use to us, either at the time or in the future.

## MEAT HASH.

Pieces of meat left from a meal, may be made into hash. Mince the meat, any kind will do, season to taste, add one minced onion, if you like it a little chopped parsley and one tablespoonful of butter; mix well, and if necessary add a little water, then place in the oven and bake brown.

## CORN BEEF HASH.

One pound of cold corned beef, minced, one dozen cold potatoes, chopped coarse; mix well together and season to taste, then add two tablespoofuls of butter and if you like, one minced onion. Bake till done.

## PORTABLE HASH.

Two pounds of cold beef, one and one-half pounds of codfish soaked and picked in small pieces, chop the meat, also twelve potatoes and mix them all together, season to taste, add a little butter and bake till sufficiently brown, add a little water to moisten. This is very nice.

## FISH HASH.

Soak and mince one pound of codfish, mash twelve potatoes, nicely mix, add four eggs well beaten, two tablespoonfuls of butter, season with salt and pepper to taste, moisten with milk and bake in a quick oven till a golden brown. Then serve.

## CODFISH AND CREAM.

Soak, shred and boil one-half pound of salt codfish; boil one quart of milk, add three tablespoonfuls of butter, and when it is hot, thicken with cornstarch or flour; have the milk thick enough to bear an egg up; then put in the fish, dust a little pepper over it, salt and four well beaten eggs added, will improve the color. Very nice for breakfast or supper.

Scraps and trimmings from meat should be saved, either for the soap grease pail, to exchange for soap, or saved to make your own soap from, as it makes very nice soft soap. Procure a can of potash and put it in some hot water, and add it boiling hot to the grease. This will be found very nice for cleaning, and easier than buying so often. This is another way in which one may save.

## STALE CAKE.

Pieces of stale cake may be made into a delightful dish in the following way: sort and trim the pieces nicely, place in a deep dish, make a boiled custard and pour over the cake. Try it.

## BREAD.

Pieces of bread may be buttered, soaked in hot milk and with a custard poured over, will make a nice bread pudding.

## SCALDS OR BURNS.

One teaspoonful of molasses, one of sweet oil and sufficient flour to make a smooth paste; dress it morning and night and apply the paste. Excellent.

## ANCHOVY TOAST.

Mix some essence of anchovy with melted butter and cut parsley, dip each slice in this and fry a golden brown.

## GERMAN TOAST.

Dip nicely sliced bread into some beaten eggs and fry in sweet, hot lard.

## FRENCH TOAST.

Toast and butter the bread and pour some hot water over it.

# GRAVIES AND SAUCES.

## BROWN GRAVY.

Made from beef stock or drippings; season with salt and pepper, cook a chopped onion with it, strain and serve with any kind of roast meat.

## DISH GRAVY.

Dish gravy is the drippings from the roast; it is not necessary to thicken it, strain and serve.

## WHITE SAUCE.

White sauce for boiled meats is made in the following way, viz:—one pint of boiling water, two tablespoonfuls of butter, thicken, season to taste and add one cup of boiling milk.

## BUTTER SAUCE.

The same as white sauce with the exception that more butter and no milk is used.

## CHICKEN OR VEAL GRAVY.

Made from the drippings in the pan in which the chicken or meat was roasted.

## GIBLET SAUCE.

Clean, wash and boil the giblets; cut them in small pieces, thicken the liquor and season it, then add the giblets, and a little chopped parsley.

## PARSLEY SAUCE.

Prepare the same as for butter sauce, season to taste, thicken and add some chopped parsley. This is nice for broiled fish or meat.

## EGG SAUCE.

The same as for butter sauce, thicken, season and add some hard boiled eggs cut in small pieces. Serve with boiled fish or fowl.

## TOMATO SAUCE.

Boil one quart of tomatoes, one minced onion, a walnut of butter; one cup of beef stock, seasoning and two tablespoonfuls of Halford sauce; strain through a coarse sieve, rub all the tomato through, then let it just come to a boil, thicken, run through a fine sieve and serve.

## SAUCE ROBERT.

Six onions, cut as for frying, three tablespoonfuls of butter, cover it to keep in the strength, after it begins to boil cover with veal broth, season to taste; when the onions are done rub through a sieve, add tomato ketchup, a little essence of burnt sugar, to color it, let it come to a boil, thicken and it will be nice with roasted game.

## VEGETABLE SAUCE.

Two medium sized carrots, one minced onion, one quart of veal broth. Boil the broth and add to it the onion, minced fine, and the carrots cut fine, and after the vegetables are done add salt and pepper to taste, Worcestershire sauce, and thicken.

## LEMON SAUCE.

Two lemons, or if extract is used, less will be required, as you might get too much alcohol, one pint of water sweetened to taste; remove the outside of the lemon, the rind, cut the lemon in quarters add to the water, also add a walnut of butter, thicken and have it real smooth, set on the back part of the stove and when ready to serve, strain. This will be good with puddings or fritters.

## VANILLA SAUCE.

One pint of hot water, sweetened to taste, a tablespoon of butter, boil and thicken and add two tablespoonfuls of vanilla, add a little salt to blend the water.

## HARD SAUCE.

One pound of nice butter, the same amount, or more of powdered sugar; mix well together, and work with the hands till it is as white as frosting; add sugar till it is as hard as you wish it, flavor with vanilla, keep in a cool place till it is wanted. When ready to serve, pour over it a cup of burnt French brandy. Serve with plum pudding.

## HOLLANDAISE SAUCE.

The yolks of six eggs, season as for mayonaise dressing, beat well and add the juice of a lemon and a little vinegar; thicken one pint of boiling water, add a walnut of butter, remove from the fire and add the mixture of eggs to it; stir as fast as you put it in and if not tart enough add more vinegar. Serve with boiled fish.

## PIQUANT SAUCE.

One pint of hot water, two tablespoonfuls of butter, one minced onion, salt and pepper to taste; boil and thicken, cut two or three cucumbers and add to it and if not sufficiently tart, add the juice of a lemon. Serve with fish or boiled meats.

## A LA TARTARE SAUCE.

One pint of boiling water, one minced onion, a walnut of butter; boil, thicken, remove from the fire and add one-half cup of capers, and two cucumber pickles, cut fine; then mix with this one cup of mayonaise dressing and the juice of one lemon. Serve with boiled salmon.

## CAPER SAUCE.

One pint of boiling water, two tablespoonsful of butter, salt to taste; boil, thicken and add two tablespoonsful of capers. Serve with boiled mutton.

## OYSTER SAUCE.

One pint of oysters, cover with water, season with salt, pepper and one tablespoonful of butter; when done, thicken and add the juice of one lemon. Serve with boiled fowl.

## GOLDEN SAUCE.

One pint of water, a walnut of butter, sweeten to taste with sugar, boil, thicken, flavor with lemon and add the yolks of four eggs to color it. Be careful not to let boil after the eggs are added.

## CREAM SAUCE.

One pint of sweetened milk or cream, boil, add one teaspoonful of butter, a little nutmeg, thicken and serve.

## WINE SAUCE.

One package of Cox's Gelatine dissolved in cold water. One pint of water, sweetened to taste; half a dozen whole spices, one cup of St. Clair wine, or any other cooking wine; have this scalding, pour over the gelatine, strain through a flannel bag, keep in a cool place till the pudding is ready to serve, and pour the wine sauce over it.

## SAUCE A LA ROYAL.

This is made the same as wine sauce, with the exception that the juice of one lemon with the yolks of two eggs, well beaten, is used for flavoring.

## BRANDY SAUCE.

One cup of good brandy, one quart of water; mix and heat scalding hot but not boiling, add one ounce of dissolved gelatine, strain and serve with plum pudding.

## LEMON SAUCE. A la Russe.

Make a nice lemon sauce; beat the whites of three eggs to a stiff froth and spread over the sauce. When ready to serve add some to every order you serve.

## SAUCE A LA FLAVOUR.

One pint of water, sugar and butter. Boil the water, add sugar to taste and a walnut of butter; after it boils add the thickening; and lemon or vanilla for flavoring.

These recipes will be found easy, if the directions are closely observed and the Author thinks there will be no trouble in making them satisfactory.

# DRESSINGS, COLORINGS AND EXTRACTS.

### SALAD DRESSING. Plain.

The yolks of four eggs, juice of one lemon and two tablespoonsful of vinegar. Break the yolks into a deep, earthern dish, beat with a wooden spoon, add mustard to taste and a teaspoonful of sweet oil, salt to taste, mix these till rather stiff and of a light golden color, then add the juice of a lemon and as much vinegar as it will bear, without making it too soft. Keep in a cool place till ready for use.

### MAYONAISE DRESSING.

Six hard boiled eggs, two lemons, one bottle of sweet oil, one teaspoonful of salt, one-half teaspoon of red pepper and one teaspoon of mustard. Mash the yolks of the eggs nicely, add two raw yolks, tablespoon of sweet oil, a little salt, dust with pepper, squeeze the juice of a lemon in it and mix very nicely and smoothly; first a little oil, then the yolk of a raw egg, and so on till it is of a light golden color; when it is mixed sufficiently add a little vinegar and mix well, then set on ice till ready for use.

### MONTIZ DRESSING.

Nearly the same as the above; one cold mashed potato is put through a collander and added to the mixture, otherwise it is the same as mayonaise dressing.

### SALAD CREAM.

Mix the ingredients the same as for mayonaise dressing and add some fresh cream. This will make it thinner and it should be placed in a glass jar, sealed and put in a cool place till it is wanted. Before using, shake well.

### SUGAR COLORING.

Colorings may be made from brown sugar, black molasses or flour and either in liquid form or in lozenge. The liquid coloring is called simidid, by the cooks that come from the West Indies. For sugar coloring; one cup of sugar, melt it and let it burn black, stir it while it is burning, when it comes to a pulp, add a little salt, pepper, allspice and put it into hot water; stir well and when it comes to a boil, cool and bottle it ready for use. Add the least little mite to the soup or gravy and it will give a brown color and will flavor also.

### MOLASSES COLORING.

Made the same way as the sugar coloring.

## FLOUR COLORING.

One cup of flour, toast it black, but not let it blaze, then add a pint of water, let it boil, strain through a very fine strainer and bottle. Be careful and not get too much in the soup as it will make it bitter.

## LOZENGE COLORING.

Burn the sugar and molasses the same as the above and when it begins to thicken, pour it into a buttered pan; it should be done as much as molasses candy is, then put in the pan, cut into small squares, and after they are sufficiently cool, wrap in fine paper. One of these will color two gallons of soup or gravy, by dropping one in, letting it dissolve and then stirring.

## CELERY EXTRACT.

For celery extract, use one pound of celery seed and one quart of water; steep this seventy-two hours, then add one pint of good rum, strain and bottle; add a teaspoon of it to the soup.

## SOY EXTRACTS.

One pound of salt, two pounds of sugar, cook half an hour over a slow fire, add three pints of boiling water, half a pint of essence of anchovy, a dozen cloves aud some sweet herbs; boil half an hour longer, then bottle. Use but a very little.

Colorings and extracts are the making of soups and gravies, and when they can be prepared at as little expense as the foregoing recipes, they should be constantly on hand, especially in restaurants and hotels.

# VEGETABLES.

The vegetables are very important in the bill of fare. Although the rest of the meal may be all that any could wish, and this part should be poorly cooked or arranged, it will detract a great deal from the meal. Care should be taken to have them well cooked (not too much, as they will break), seasoned lightly, as they may be seasoned more at the table. One should know the time required to boil the different kinds; there are some who, should you ask them how long potatoes need to boil, would be unable to tell you. Vegetables as well as the other parts of the meal should be prepared and served in an agreeable manner.

## BOILED POTATOES.

Wash and pare the potatoes, put them into the kettle with hardly enough water to cover (the water should be cold), and when the water boils, add a tablespoon of salt; boil fifteen or twenty minutes and they are done; drain the water off and keep on the back of the stove till time to serve them; then peel and send to the table. If the potatoes are old they will require ten minutes longer.

## MASHED POTATOES.

Pare and boil the potatoes till just done; then mash them, season with salt and pepper to taste, and add as much milk or cream as is necessary, mix well and heap the vegetable dish high with them and serve. Do not pack the potatoes into the dish.

## FRIED POTATOES. Plain.

Slice some cold boiled potatoes, drop them into hot lard or drippings and fry brown. Sprinkle a little salt over them and serve.

## FRENCH FRIED POTATOES.

Pare some potatoes and cut them into long, small, three-cornered pieces; keep them in water until you are ready to cook them; drop them into hot lard, fry quickly and brown, drain in a collander and serve.

## SARATOGA POTATOES.

Cut some raw potatoes into wafers and fry crisp in hot fat, sprinkle a little salt over them and serve. Do not let them soak in the fat.

## GRIDDLED POTATOES.

Cut some cold, boiled potatoes into slices, broil over a hot fire, sprinkle a little salt over them and add a little butter and serve hot.

## STEWED POTATOES.

Cut some raw potatoes into small square pieces, having first peeled them, cover with hot water and boil. When they are done, drain off the water, cover with hot milk, add salt, pepper and a little butter, thicken a little, and to improve the flavor, sprinkle a little chopped parsley over the top and serve.

## POTATO TURNIPS.

Pare, cook and mash six potatoes, as for mashed potatoes; boil an equal amount of turnips, mash and season, then mix the two together and it will be an addition to a turkey dinner.

## QUEEN POTATOES.

Boil the potatoes, have them very firm, then dip them into a beaten egg, drop them into a kettle of fat and fry brown. Send to the table covered with a napkin.

## ESCALLOPED POTATOES.

Season some mashed potatoes to taste; put a layer of this in a baking dish, then a layer of slices of hard boiled eggs, and so on. Spread butter over the top and bake a golden brown. Serve in the same dish.

## POTATO SALAD.

Cut six potatoes in squares, one minced onion, a little chopped parsley or celery, salt and pepper to taste one-half a cup of sweet oil and vinegar to taste. Put into a dish and garnish with red beets.

## STUFFED TOMATOES.

With a sharp knife, remove the stem end of the tomatoes, take out the inside of them; place the shells of tomatoes into a pan about one-half an inch apart; mix the inside part with cracker or bread crumbs, about one-third crumbs, so it will be quite stiff, salt and pepper add a little butter to taste; fill the shells with this, replace the tops and bake in a moderate oven.

## STEWED TOMATOES.

If canned ones are used, season with salt, pepper, butter and a little sugar; then stew.

If fresh ones are used; put them into boiling water in order to remove the skins more easily, slice, stew in the juice, season to taste with salt, pepper, a little butter and if necessary, add some crumbs.

## SALAD D'TOMATO.

Slice the tomatoes nicely, lay them in an oval dish, pour vinegar and salt over them and send to the table.

## ESCALLOPED TOMATOES.

Place some slices of tomatoes in the bottom of a baking pan, then a dust of cracker crumbs, a little salt, pepper and butter, and so on till you have a sufficient quantity; the last layer should be of crumbs, then bake till done.

## BOILED HOMINY.

One cup of hominy, or as much as you think you will need; soak over night; next morning put into a small dish or basin, with enough water to cook it, and set this in a larger dish of hot water, so that it will not burn. When done add salt and serve with cold cream or fresh milk.

## STRING BEANS.

Remove the strings from the beans, cut or break them into small pieces, cover with water and boil; add a piece of salt pork to the water, as it improves the flavor. When tender remove the pork, add salt, butter to taste, drain off most of the water and serve.

## BAKED BEANS.

One quart of white beans, one and one-half pounds of salt pork. Soak the beans over night in cold water, the water should cover them entirely, and more too, then in the morning drain the water from them, put the beans into a bean pot; score the pork in little squares in the rind, place in the centre of the beans. Put in water enough to cover them, a little salt and bake in a moderate oven; replace the water as it boils away, bake till done and serve.

## BOSTON BAKED BEANS.

One quart of beans and two pounds of salt pork; soak the beans over night; then drain them, place half of them in the bean pot, then put the scored pork in the centre, add the rest of the beans, three tablespoonsful of molasses, cover with water and bake in a moderate oven, adding water as it boils away. Cook till done and serve Sunday morning with Boston plum brown bread.

## LIMA BEANS.

One quart of fresh shelled Lima beans, wash, cover with water and boil ; add a piece of salt pork, when done add salt and pepper to taste; remove the pork and serve.

## SPINACH. Southern way.

One peck of spinach, remove all the dried leaves and the roots, boil and add two pounds of salt pork; cook gently, add salt and butter to taste and serve. All the water should have been previously drained from the spinach.

## SPINACH. Northern way.

One peck of spinach boiled with two pounds of salt pork; boil gently, drain off all the water, and mix with the spinach two dozen hard boiled eggs, cut very fine; add salt and butter to taste.

## SUCCOTASH.

Boil one quart of corn taken from the cob, and also a pint of purple shelled beans; when done, drain the water from the beans, mix the corn and beans, season to taste with salt and butter and serve.

## CORN.

If green corn is used, remove all the husks and silk from the ears, and boil twenty minutes in water lightly salted, and serve.

If canned corn is used, stew it five minutes, add salt and butter to taste and some boiled milk; then serve.

## TURNIPS.

Pare and wash as many turnips as you wish, boil till tender, drain off the water, mash and season as you would potatoes.

## CREAM TURNIPS.

Pare one quart of turnips, cut them in squares, cover with water, boil till done; thicken with cornstarch, season to taste, add one cup of cream or sweet milk. Very nice with roast lamb.

# BREAD.

We should all understand how to make good bread. Any meal is not complete without good bread. We do not care to eat bread that is not baked sufficiently, or sour, soggy bread. What we want is nice white, spongy bread; it should be fine celled too, and it is not every one that is able to make such bread. It is indeed an accomplishment to be able to make nice bread. A cook will be able to obtain a better situation if he is able to make good bread as well as being a good meat cook.

## WHITE BREAD.

One quart of water, one quart of milk, one ounce of compressed yeast, one ounce of butter and one ounce of salt; add flour and mix well together till quite stiff; let it stand five hours and knead, using as little flour as possible, let it rise one hour and bake.

## GRAHAM BREAD. No. 1.

One quart of warm water, one cup of wheat flour, one cup of indian meal, one cup of yeast, one teaspoonful of molasses and one-half teaspoonful of salt, also of saleratus, add sufficient graham meal to mix well; rise over night, mix and rise once more and bake.

## GRAHAM BREAD. No. 2.

Two quarts of yeast, one quart of warm water, flour to make a sponge. When the sponge has risen enough, add twelve quarts of water, warm, three pints of molasses and four ounces of salt dissolved in the water. Mix the sponge well with the molasses and water, add equal quantities of graham and white flour and make quite stiff. Let it rise three-quarters of an hour, mould into loaves, rise again and bake in a medium oven.

## GRAHAM BREAD. No. 3.

Five quarts of water, two ounces of compressed yeast, dissolved in the water, flour to make a sponge. When the sponge is light add three quarts of water, six ounces of salt, two quarts of molasses, equal quantities of graham and white flour, make a stiff dough; let it rise one-half of an hour, mould, rise twenty minutes and bake.

## WHITE BREAD. Baker's Yeast.

Three quarts of yeast, two quarts of water, flour for a sponge. When ready, add three quarts of water, six ounces of salt, one-quarter of a pound of butter or lard, one-quarter of a pound of sugar, flour to mix quite stiff. Let it rise one-half of an hour, mould into loaves or biscuit, rise and bake. The butter should be melted.

## WHITE BREAD. Compressed Yeast.

Five quarts of water, two ounces of compressed yeast, dissolved in the water, one-quarter of a pound of butter or lard, three ounces of salt, one-quarter of a pound of sugar and flour to mix quite stiff Set it to rise for three hours, knead; rise twenty minutes, mould into loaves, rise one half of an hour and bake.

J. GIBSON.

## HOP YEAST.

Ten quarts of water, four ounces of hops; add the hops to the hot water and boil slowly one-half of an hour; then strain and mix three-quarters of a pound of flour with a sufficient quantity of the water in which the hops were boiled, to mix into a stiff batter; add one pint of dry malt to the rest of the liquid and mix with the batter. Cool and add one pint of old hop yeast and cover air-tight. Let it set thirty-six hours and it is ready for use. Keep in a cool place and cover air-tight.

## POTATO YEAST.

One-half peck of boiled potatoes; mash them and mix with them two pounds of flour. To fifteen quarts of cool water add three pints of hop yeast; cover tightly and set for twelve hours, strain off the top till you have five quarts remaining; add the liquid to the potatoes, keep in a cool place; it should be covered very tightly till wanted for use. To the five quarts left in the dish, add five quarts of water and keep to set a sponge. Then to this sponge add eight quarts of water, one-half pound of salt and one-half pound of butter or lard, mix well, flour to mix stiff and it will make nice bread or biscuits.

These yeasts are suitable for hotels, restaurants or private families. The quantity may be increased or diminished as you wish.

## BOSTON BROWN BREAD.

Two-thirds Indian meal, one-third rye meal; mix together dry. Six quarts of cool water, three pints of molasses, four ounces of salt dissolved in water, two ounces of saleratus and one quart of potato yeast; this to be made into a light batter. Whatever quantity you wish to make let it stand one-half hour after mixing. Put into pans and bake in a medium heated oven, or steam. J. G.

## NEW ENGLAND BROWN BREAD.

Two-thirds Indian meal, one-third rye meal; mix dry. Seven quarts of water, three pints of molasses added to the water, the water to be cool; four ounces of salt dissolved in the water, two ounces of saleratus, two ounces of compressed yeast dissolved into a pint of warm water, and strain into the liquid mixture, let it stand ten minutes, then put into pans and bake in a moderate oven from eight to ten hours. For this quantity add three pounds of raisins.

J. G.

## CREAM TARTAR BISCUIT.

Two and one-half ounces cream of tartar mixed with five pounds of flour, two quarts of milk, one and one-half ounces of saleratus and one and one-half ounces of salt dissolved in a portion of the milk, four ounces of butter, melted, and mix into the dough. In working this mixture dust it with flour. Cut out and bake in a quick oven. J. GIBSON.

## WHEAT MUFFINS. No. 1.

Four and one-half pounds of flour, two quarts of milk, two and one-half ounces of cream of tartar mixed into the dry flour, one and one-half ounces of soda, one and one-half ounces of salt dissolved in the milk, six ounces of sugar, four ounces of melted butter and five eggs. These ingredients are to be made into a light batter, dipped out and put into muffin rings; bake in a quick oven.

J. GIBSON.

## GRAHAM MUFFINS. No. 2.

Two-thirds white flour, one-third graham, with the equal proportion of ingredients mentioned in the above recipe.

J. GIBSON.

## PROFESSOR BRAXTON'S SALLY LUNN.

One quart of flour, three eggs, milk enough to mix to a smooth batter as for griddle cakes. Break the eggs and mix well together, add three tablespoonsful of melted butter, half a cup of sugar and three teaspoonsful of baking powder; put into shallow pans and bake in a medium heated oven; let it rise, then cook to a light brown. Serve hot for breakfast. Add salt to taste. Use one and one-half inch cake pans for this mixture.

## STOCK YEAST.

One pail of water, four ounces of hops, one quart of malt and one-half pound of flour. Let the water boil, add the hops. Take about a quart of the boiling hop water and pour over the flour, working the flour through with a stick for that purpose. Boil the rest of the hop water about fifteen minutes and strain it on the scalded flour, then let it remain one half hour; then add the malt and let it stand until the heat of the hop water is about ninety degrees; never go above that as it is apt to sour; always use a thermometer. Take one quart of stock yeast from the last brewing, or buy it at the bakers, or make it yourself by taking two quarts of water, two ounces of hops, one pint of malt and three ounces of flour; make the same as stock yeast. Let it stand in a glass jar, for at least thirty-six hours. A thick foam will rise on top before it is ready for use. Take a quart of it to stock your stock yeast, which must stand thirty hours before it is ready for use. Always keep a quart of this yeast to stock the next brewing.

Ferment is what I make every night, to put into dough. Boil about one-fourth of a pail of potatoes and put them into a tub, add one pound of strong flour and pound them well together Take one pail of water and pour over the potatoes and flour, and blend them well together. Have the heat about ninety degrees. Add about one quart of stock yeast, and stir together. This ferment will be ready for use in about fourteen hours.

To make a home made dough, take three fourths of a pail of water, three-fourths of a pail of ferment, strained, twelve ounces of salt, four ounces of sugar and one pound of lard. Mix a fair sized dough and let stand about four hours. Beat it down with the hands and let stand one-half an hour in dough, then put into pans.

For sponge or baker's bread, take one-half a pail of ferment, and one-fourth a pail of water, ninety degrees in winter, less in summer; mix lightly and let it stand about four hours, or until it drops one-half an inch; then take three-fourths of a pail of water, twelve ounces of salt, four ounces of sugar and one pound of lard, and mix with flour till stiff enough for bread dough. Let it stand one hour, knead, then one-half hour longer, and put into pans. I give this recipe just as I work it myself.

ED. LEWIS, Baker.

## TEA BISCUIT.

Two quarts of the liquid, that is, when you have everything except flour; add two ounces of sugar, two ounces of lard and one ounce of compressed yeast. Mix as usual for biscuit; mould, and make into rolls as the above mentioned.

## JOHNNY CAKE. No. 1.

One pint of Indian meal and one-half pint of white flour, mix the meal and flour together dry, add a little salt and one-half a cup of melted butter; mix with milk to a smooth medium batter; four eggs, well mixed, four tablespoonsful of baking powder and a little sugar. Bake in a quick oven to a golden brown.

## JOHNNY CAKE. No. 2.

One pint of Indian meal and four eggs; mix to a batter with milk, add three and one-half tablespoonsful of baking powder. Have a hot gridiron and cook in butter as you would griddle cakes. Serve in a napkin, hot.

## GRAHAM GEMS.

One-half pint of graham flour, one pint of white flour, four eggs, one-half cup of melted butter and salt to season. Mix the graham and white flour together, add the eggs and butter and four teaspoonsful of baking powder. Have the gem moulds warm and well greased with butter, or lard. Bake in a medium hot oven until cooked.

White gems can be made as the above recipe by adding the same ingredients without the graham meal.

Corn cake can be made the same as Johnny cake No. 1, by adding the same, according to the quantity you want to make. Mix, put into muffin rings and bake in a medium hot oven.

## PASTE YEAST.

Put six ounces of good hops into one pail of boiling water; let this boil fifteen minutes, strain; take fourteen pounds of strong flour and pour the boiling hop water over it, stirring with a stick, until it is smooth and stiff; set it away in a cool place. When you want to make your stock, take one and one-half pounds of the paste, two quarts of water, one quart of malt and two ounces of compressed yeast; set it away at ninety degrees heat. It will be ready in twelve hours. When it is ready, set the ferment; that is, boil one-fourth of a pail of potatoes, throw them into a tub, and add one and one-half pounds of flour, one and one half pails of water and one-half of the stock; put in the ferment and it will be ready in about twelve or fifteen hours. To the other half of the stock, add one quart of water, one quart of malt and three pints of paste; set away as usual. When you want to make the stock a little stronger, add a little more malt and paste. Make the dough and sponge the same as liquid stock yeast. A splendid ferment can be made by boiling one-fourth of a pail of potatoes, pounding into it, when boiled, one and one-half pounds of flour; add a pail and one-half of water and three ounces of compressed yeast. Work the same as the other mentioned.

Mr. ED. LEWIS, Baker.

## A GOOD HOME-MADE YEAST.

Boil two quarts of water and three ounces of hops. Take eight good sized potatoes, peel, and let them remain in the strained hop-water until cooked. Take one quart of blended flour, and strain the potato hop water on it, mixing it well. Add one cup of sugar and one ounce of salt; let it stand until cool enough to add one cake of compressed yeast, or one cup of baker's yeast. Be sure to keep a cup of your yeast bottled away for the next brewing. House-keepers will find this to be a very good way of making yeast.

Mrs. ED. LEWIS.

## CREAM TARTAR BISCUIT.

Three pounds of good St. Louis flour, one quart of sweet milk, a quarter of a pound of lard, two ounces of salt, one ounce of soda and two and one-half ounces of cream tartar. Rub the flour and lard together, make a hole in the centre of the flour and put in the cream tartar and salt, mix the soda into the milk, and mix the dough smooth as for bread. Roll out about one and one half inches thick, cut out and put into greased pans. Bake in a quick oven.

ED. LEWIS.

## CORN-MEAL MUSH.

Eight pounds of corn flour and one pound of salt, scald gradually with boiling water until like a batter. I use this quantity to about two buckets of water. For making a less quantity, judge accordingly. This mixture is to put into home-made bread. It is generally the rule to add this corn flour mush to the dough, after it is mixed according to the quantity you are going to make, to give the bread its regular weight. It will be found to be very healthful and palatable.

Mr. ED. LEWIS, Baker.

## VIENNA BREAD.

Three ounces of compressed yeast, three ounces of salt, one-half gallon of milk, one-half gallon of water and four ounces of lard. Mix like a good batter and let it stand till almost dropping, say about four hours; then mix flour enough in to make like a roll dough, let it stand about one hour, then roll out long and pointed at the ends. Place in cloth, with a layer of cloth between each loaf. When raised enough, place on pans, and with a sharp knife cut three strokes across; wash with a little scalded flour before cutting, to give the gloss. Bake until a nice brown. Make a little steam in the oven by throwing in a little water, to keep it nice and soft.

## VIENNA ROLLS.

Use the same mixture with the addition of about four ounces of sugar. Take about one and one-half ounces of dough and mould it round, let it stand until soft; then take a wooden rolling pin and roll out long. With the palm of your hand fold it in towards you. Put into pans a little apart, wash with milk, bake in a nice, brisk oven.

ED. LEWIS.

## RYE BREAD.

When the sponge is ready, take, for ten or twelve loaves of bread, four pounds of sponge and two quarts of liquid sponge, mix in one-half rye flour and one-half white flour; make to about the same consistency of biscuit dough. Put into pans dusted with corn meal, let it remain in the closet until raised enough, be careful and not let it rise too much; when it is about half risen, wash, cut and put gently into a hot oven. Before baking the white bread, wash with water.

ED. LEWIS, Baker.

## GRAHAM BREAD.

Mix similar to white bread, only use graham flour and a little molasses to color brown.                               ED. LEWIS.

## OAT MEAL BREAD.

Scald two pounds of oat meal until nice and soft, and add about twelve eggs.    Biscuit can be made out of this dough if wished.                                              ED. LEWIS.

## BOSTON BROWN BREAD.

One bushel of Indian meal, one half bushel of rye meal, five quarts of molasses, thirty ounces of salt, ten ounces of saleratus, five pints of ferment yeast or five ounces of compressed yeast, five pounds of strong flour and five small pails of water.    Bake in a cool oven all night, or it can be steamed, if wished.    First, mix the flour and meal together and add one of the pails of water, then add the salt and another pail of water, molasses next, then saleratus, then yeast.    With the last the water must be added by degrees, as it may not need all of it.    Bake in a cool oven (baker's if possible), for six or seven hours.    If a baker's oven is not convenient, it can be steamed the same as plum pudding.    This is a regular baker's recipe, but it can be reduced down to the smallest quantity that is wished to be made.                                       ED. LEWIS.

## SOUTHERN WAY OF MAKING BREAD.

Persons who have not traveled in the South may think it somewhat strange how they make their bread so plain, yet so wholesome, palatable and digestible.    As I am familiar with the way of preparing the different kinds of bread of the South, I will give a few of the leading recipes.

## WHITE INDIAN MEAL CORN CAKE.

This recipe is made without any rising or soda to make it light. Three pints of white corn meal, season with salt, mix it with cold water to a smooth dough, put into pans and bake in a hot oven until baked.

In the South this bread is baked in what is called spiders, on an open hearth, with hot coals on the top and bottom, and which stands on three legs.

## INDIAN MEAL RAISED BREAD.

Three pints of Indian meal, one and one-half home-made yeast cakes dissolved in water and a little salt.    Mix the meal in a pan or tray, make a hole in the centre and pour in the yeast, mix it with sour milk; let it stand in the pan over night, in the morning, bake in a medium hot oven.    This will be found to be very nice for breakfast.

## INDIAN MEAL SWEET BREAD.

Make the same as the above recipe, only add sugar in mixing:

## INDIAN MEAL HOE CAKE.

One pint of Indian meal, a little salt and one egg. Mix with milk or luke-warm water to a smooth batter. Cook on a gridiron for breakfast.

## SOUTHERN LOAF BREAD.

One quart of flour and one cup of potato yeast; mix with milk. Mix well a little salt and a little melted lard into the flour before adding the yeast; mix to a stiff dough, put into a pan and cover; let it stand until morning, then make into small loaves and bake in a medium hot oven. This is generally served on a napkin at the breakfast table.

Southern raised biscuit are made in the same way as the loaf bread mentioned.

## SOUTHERN RAISIN BREAD OR BISCUIT.

One quart of flour, one and one-half cakes of home-made yeast, one large tablespoonful of melted lard mixed well with the flour and a little salt. Make a hole in the centre of the flour; dissolve the yeast cake in warm water, and pour into it; mix with cold water to a stiff dough; add one cup of stoned raisins, mix and set in a warm place; when raised, mould into loaves or biscuits. Bake in a medium hot oven.

## BUTTER MILK BISCUITS.

One quart of flour, two tablespoonsful of cream tartar, one teaspoonful of soda dissolved in a cup of milk, one tablespoonful of melted lard and salt to season. Mix the cream tartar in the dry flour; then mix the flour with fresh butter to a medium dough. Bake in a quick oven.

## CRACKLING BREAD OR BISCUIT.

One quart of flour, a little salt, two cups of cracklings or scraps of crisp, fresh pork well mixed; add cream tartar and soda as mentioned in the above recipe. Mix with milk and bake in a brisk oven for breakfast.

## CRACKLING CORN CAKE.

Make in the same way as crackling wheat meal biscuit.

## GRAHAM GEMS.

Two eggs, one cup of sweet milk, one cup of cold milk, two cups of unsifted graham flour and one tablespoonful of sugar. Bake three-quarters of an hour.

# GENERAL REMARKS ABOUT CAKE.

## CURRANT CAKE.

Six eggs, one pound of butter, one and one-half pounds of sugar, one pound of flour and one-half pound of currants. Rub the butter and sugar together, being careful not to rub them so much as to make them greasy; when these are rubbed smooth, add the eggs, work very lightly, adding one or two at a time; as you work in the eggs add the two cups of milk; then the flour with two teaspoonsful of baking powder added; then work in the currants last. Bake to a golden brown in a very moderate oven.

## CURRANT CAKE. No. 2.

Six eggs, one pound of sugar, one pound of butter, one cup of currants, two pounds of flour and two teaspoonsful of baking powder. Mix the sugar and butter together, then add two cups of milk, flour, baking powder and currants last. After the ingredients are all carefully mixed together put into pans and bake in a moderate oven.

## TO BLANCH ALMONDS.

Put almonds into a sauce pan with plenty of cold water and heat slowly. When the water is just scalding, turn the almonds into a basin, peel, and throw them into cold water; dry them well in soft cloth before they are used. If the water is too hot it will turn them yellow.

## TO POUND ALMONDS.

Almonds are more easily pounded and less liable to become oily if dried in a gentle degree of heat after they are blanched; left, for example, in a warm room for two or three days, lightly spread on a large dish or tin. They should be sprinkled during the heating with a few drops of cold water, the white of an egg or the juice of a lemon and pounded to a smooth paste. This is more easily done, we believe, when first roughly chopped, but we prefer to have them thrown at once into the mortar.

## TO REDUCE ALMONDS TO A PASTE.

Chop them a little on a large and very clean trencher, then with a paste roller (rolling-pin) roll them well until no small bits are perceptible among them. We have found this method admirable, but as some of the oil is pressed from the almonds by it and absorbed by the board, we would recommend a marble slab as preferable. Should they be intended for a sweet dish, sugar should be strewed under them. When a board or strong trencher is used, it should be rather higher in the middle than at the sides.

## TO COLOR ALMONDS FOR CAKE OR PASTRY.

Blanch, dry and chop them a little, pour a prepared cochineal into the hands and roll the almonds between them until they are equally colored, then spread them on a sheet of paper and place them in a very gentle degree of heat to dry. Use spinach juice for coloring green, and a strong infusion of saffron to give them a yellow tint. They have a pretty effect when strewed over icing tarts, or cakes, especially the rose-colored ones, which should be very pale.

## TO PREPARE BUTTER FOR RICH CAKE.

For all large and very rich cakes the usual directions are, to beat the butter to a cream; but we find they are quite as light, and more so, when it is cut small and gently melted with just as much heat as will dissolve it, and no more. If it be shaken around in a pan, previously warmed, and held near the fire for a short time, it will soon be liquified, which is all that is required. It must on no account be hot when it is added to the other ingredients, to which it must be poured in small portions after they are all mixed, in the way which we have minutely described in the recipe for Maderia cakes and that of the Sutherland pudding. To cream it, drain the water well from it after it is cut; soften it a little before the fire. Should it be very hard, beat it with the back of a large wooden spoon till it resembles thick cream. When prepared thus, the sugar is added to it first and then the other ingredients in succession.

## TO WHISK EGGS FOR LIGHT, RICH CAKE.

Break them one by one and separate the yolks from the whites; this is easily done by pouring the yolk from one-half of the shell to the other and letting the whites drop from it into a basin beneath. With a small three-pronged fork remove the specks from each egg as it is broken, that none may accidently escape notice. Whisk the yolks until they appear light, and the whites until they are quite a solid froth, while any liquid remains at the bottom of the bowl, they are not sufficiently beaten. When a portion of them, taken up with the whisk and dropped from it, remain standing in points, they are in the proper state for use, and should be mixed in the cake directly.

## ORANGE-FLOWER MACAROONS.

Have ready two pounds of very dry, white sifted sugar; weigh two ounces of the petals of freshly gathered orange blossoms, after they have been picked from the stems; cut them very small with a pair of scissors into the sugar, as they will become discolored if not mixed quickly after they are cut. When all are done, add the whites of seven eggs and beat the whole well together till it looks like snow; then drop the mixture upon paper without delay, and send the cakes to a very cool oven.

Two pounds of pounded sugar, two ounces orange blossoms and the whites of seven eggs. Bake twenty minutes or more.

It is almost impossible to state with accuracy the precise time required for these cakes, so much depends on the oven. They should be very delicately colored, yet dried through.

## ALMOND MACAROONS.

Blanch a pound of fresh Jordan almonds, wipe them dry and set them in a very cool oven to render them perfectly so; pound them to an exceedingly smooth paste with a little white of egg; then whisk to a firm, solid froth the whites of seven eggs, or eight, if they are small; mix with them one and one-half pounds of the finest sugar; add these by degrees to the almonds; whisk the whole up well together and drop the mixture upon a wafer paper, which may be procured at the confectioners. Bake in a moderate oven to a very pale brown.

It is an improvement to the flavor of these cakes to substitute an ounce of bitter almonds for one of the sweet. They are sometimes made with an equal weight of each; and another variety of them is obtained by gently browning the almonds in a slow oven before they are pounded.

One pound of Jordan almonds, blanched; one and one-half pounds of sugar and the whites of seven or eight eggs. Fifteen to twenty minutes.

## IMPERIALS.

Work into a pound of sifted flour six ounces of butter, and mix well with them half a pound of sifted sugar, six ounces of currants, two ounces of candied orange peel, the grated rind of one lemon, and four well-beaten eggs. Flour a tin lightly, and with a couple of forks place the paste upon it in small, rough heaps, about two inches apart. Bake them in a very gentle oven from fifteen to twenty minutes or until they are colored a pale brown.

## SMALL RICH CAKES.

Four eggs, one-half pound of sugar, four ounces of butter, four ounces of flour and lemon peel, mace or cinnamon. Bake fifteen minutes.

Beat and mix well together four eggs properly whisked and one-half pound of powdered sugar. Pour to them by degrees, three-fourths of a pound of clarified butter, a little cool, stir lightly in with these four ounces of dried, sifted flour. Beat the mixture about fifteen minutes, then put into a small buttered patty-pan and bake in a medium oven about fifteen minutes.

They should be flavored with the rasp or the grated peel of a small lemon or with pounded mace or cinnamon.

## ROACHED ALMONDS.

Eight ounces of almonds, six ounces of candied orange peel, one ounce of citron, two ounces of flour, three-fourths of a pound of sugar, one teaspoonful of cinnamon and mace, mixed, and whites of three large eggs. Bake in a medium heated oven twenty minutes.

Chop together very fine eight ounces of almonds, blanched and dried; six ounces of candied orange peel, or of orange or lemon peel, mixed, and one ounce of citron. Add to them two ounces of flour; three-quarters of a pound of sugar, a small teaspoonful of cinnamon or mace and the whites of three large eggs. Roll the mixture into balls about the size of a large marble. Bake them on wafer paper twenty minutes in a medium oven. They should be very crisp, but not deeply colored.

When the flavor is not disliked it will be found an improvement to substitute an ounce of the bitter almonds for one of the sweet; and we prefer the whole of the almonds and candied peel also, cut into spikes instead of being chopped. The ingredients must then be made into light paste, and placed in small heaps on the paper.

## BITTER ALMOND BISCUIT.

Blanch and chop as fine as possible two ounces of bitter almonds and add them to one-half a pound of flour, half a pound of sifted sugar and two ounces of butter, well mixed together. Whisk the whites of two eggs to a stiff froth and beat them lightly with the other ingredients. Drop the cakes on a buttered tin or copper oven leaf and bake rather slowly from ten to twelve minutes. They should be very small. Should the proportion of bitter almonds be considered unhealthful, use one-half as many, and substitute sweet ones for the remainder.

One-half a pound of flour, one-half a pound of sugar, two ounces of butter, two ounces of bitter almonds and the whites of two eggs.

## A NICE ALMOND CAKE.

Blanch, dry and pound to the finest possible paste, eight ounces of fresh, Jordan almonds and one ounce of bitter; moisten with a few drops of water or white of an egg to prevent oiling; then mix with them, very gradually, twelve fresh eggs, which have been whisked until they are exceedingly light; throw in, by degrees, one pound of dry sifted sugar, constantly stirring the mixture, as the separate ingredients are added, with a large wooden spoon. Mix in, by degrees, three-fourths of a pound of dry flour, of the best quality; then pour in gently a pound of butter, which has just been melted but not allowed to become hot, and beat it very gradually and thoroughly into the cake, letting one portion entirely disappear before another is thrown in; add the rasp, or the finely grated rind of two sound, fresh lemons; fill a thickly buttered mould rather more than half full of the mixture. Bake it from one and one half to two hours in a well heated oven. Lay a paper over the top when sufficiently colored and carefully guard against burning.

One-half a pound of sweet almonds, one ounce of bitter almonds, twelve eggs, one pound of sugar, three-quarters of a pound of flour, one pound of butter and the rind of two lemons.

### DROP CAKE. No. 1.

One pound of sugar, six ounces of lard or butter, one-half ounce of soda, one-half ounce of ammonia or cream tartar, three pints of sour milk and four eggs ; flavor with extract of lemon.

Rub the lard or butter with the sugar in a wooden bowl; always rub less with lard than butter. When lard is used a little salt is needed to be added. Blend the soda in the milk and pour on the butter; pound the ammonia in an iron pestle; then pour all in, mix with flour sufficient to make a batter so as to pass through a bag. Drop them about the size of an egg; separate on a greased pan and bake in a hot oven. If cream tartar is used, you must use sweet milk and sift the cream tartar with the flour. Baking powder can be used, if wished, and put into the flour in the same way.

Mr. ED. LEWIS.

### DROP CAKES. No. 2.

One-half pound of sugar, one-fourth pound of butter, two eggs, one pound of sifted flour, one-fourth ounce of soda, one-half ounce of cream tartar or two spoonsful of baking powder, one-half gill of sweet milk. Rub the butter and sugar together, add the eggs by degrees, then the milk, extract of lemon and the powder mixed with the flour. Bake in a quick oven. Drop with a finger bag the same as first. Add a few currants if wished.

### DROP CAKES. No. 3.

One and one-half pounds of sugar, three-quarters of a pound of butter and lard, mixed, one gill of eggs; one quart and one gill of milk, one-half ounce of saleratus, one ounce of cream tartar or same of baking powder, two and three-quarter pounds of flour or enough to make into a stiff batter, a little mace and oil of lemon. Bake the same as the above. E. L.

### JUMBLES. No. 1.

One pound of sugar, one pound of butter, three pounds of eggs, two pounds of flour (strong), one-half teaspoonful of lemon and one-fourth ounce of baking powder or ammonia. Place in the machine, and flour the board that runs underneath, and the mixture will run out on the board in three long strings. Take a knife and cut the strings about four inches long, put each piece in the shape of a circle and press the ends together and put into pans. If you have no machine cut with cutters.

## JUMBLES. No. 2, Middling.

One pound of sugar, one-half pound of butter, five eggs, one-half gill of milk, two pounds of flour, one-fourth ounce of baking powder or ammonia, pound it in a mortar and mix in the milk, baking powder and flour. Stir, then cut or use the machine.

## JUMBLES. No. 3, Cheap.

One pound of sugar, one-half pound of butter, five eggs, one gill of milk, one-fourth ounce of baking powder or ammonia, two pounds and two ounces of flour and extract of lemon. Bake in a good hot oven. E. L.

## VANILLA SNAPS.

One-half pound of granulated sugar, one-half pound of butter and six eggs. Mix the sugar, butter and eggs together, with extract of vanilla to flavor; then add enough flour to make a light batter. Grease the pans lightly, and with a spoon drop in one-half spoonful, apart, so as not to touch; spread with the back of the spoon a little, and bake until a golden brown.

## GINGER SNAPS.

One quart of molasses, a pinch of salt, one ounce of ginger, two ounces of soda, twelve ounces of lard and one pound of granulated sugar. Add the sugar last. Make it stiff enough to roll out. Cut with cutters and bake.

## LEMON SNAPS.

Two and one-half pounds of sugar, eight eggs, two pounds and ten ounces of flour, one pound of butter, extract of lemon, one and one-fourth teaspoonsful of baking powder, or the same of soda and cream tartar—one part soda and two parts cream tartar. Bake in a moderate oven. E. L.

## SPONGE CAKE. No. 1.

One pound of sugar, twelve eggs, one pound of flour and a few drops of vanilla. Beat the sugar and eggs well for twenty minutes.

## SPONGE CAKE. No. 2.

The same mixture as No. 1. Separate the whites from the yolks. Beat the yolks and sugar well together, and the whites till stiff enough to cut with a knife. Put the whites and beaten yolks together and mix carefully; when well mixed add the flour. Bake in a slow oven.

## LADY FINGERS.

Use the same mixture as for sponge cake only put into a finger bag, and drop on papers, fitted into pans; when cooked, turn the papers over and wet them with water to remove the cake from the paper.

## QUEEN JELLY CAKE.

Use the same mixture as for sponge cake. Spread in shallow pans and bake in a medium oven. Spread the mixture in pans about one-half an inch thick. When baked spread jam in the centre and frost the top with white frosting; then put chocolate frosting in a bag and run it up and down over the white frosting; then take a fork and spread it crosswise.

## WINE CAKE.

One and one-half pounds of sugar, one pound of butter, two and one-half pounds of flour, seventeen eggs, one-half a pint of milk, one-half ounce of soda and one ounce of cream tartar. Mix the butter and sugar well together and add the eggs, by degrees, two or three at a time. Dissolve the soda in milk and add to the other ingredients; add the flour, well mixed with the cream tartar.

## SPICE CAKE.

One quart of molasses, one pint of milk, two ounces of soda, two ounces of spice, four and one-half pounds of flour and three-quarters of a pound of lard. Mix the molasses, milk, soda, spice and lard together, then add the flour. If for cut cake, bake in hot oven; if loaf cake, bake in slow oven.

## LEMON WAFERS.

Six pounds of flour, four pounds of sugar, two pounds of butter, two ounces of ammonia and fifteen eggs. Mix the butter and sugar together. Pound the ammonia and put the eggs on top; mix well and add the other ingredients. Add the flour last. Two spoonsful of cream tartar and one of soda can be used instead of the ammonia, if preferred.

## POUND CAKE.

One pound and three ounces of sugar, one pound of butter, one and one-fourth pounds of flour and twelve eggs. Mix the sugar and butter together; and the eggs by degrees; then mix in the flour. Flavor with mace.

## HARD GINGER BREAD AND GINGER NUTS.

One quart of molasses, one pound of lard, one pint of milk, two ounces of soda and four and one-half pounds of flour. Put the ginger into the molasses, and mix the molasses and lard together; dissolve the soda in the milk, then add the flour. Bake in a medium oven.

Take this same mixture to make New York ginger nuts. Mould the mixture into balls, the size of an egg, and flatten them with the hand; then with a milk can top dipped into flour, flatten them again. Brush over the top with the beaten yolk of egg mixed with a little milk.

## GINGER SQUARES.

One quart of molasses, one-half pint of milk, one pound of sugar, twelve ounces of butter, one ounce of soda and five pounds of flour. Add the ginger to the molasses and mix the butter, molasses and sugar together; dissolve the soda in the milk, and add the flour last. After it is well mixed, roll out thin and cut with a square cutter. Put on to pans, wash over with the egg and bake in a medium oven.

## BRIGHTON CAKE.

Four and one-half pounds of sugar, three pounds of butter, three ounces of ammonia, or two ounces of cream tartar and one of soda, three eggs, one pint of milk and ten and one half pounds of flour. Mix the sugar and butter well together and add the eggs by degrees. Dissolve the soda in the milk and add to the sugar and butter. If ammonia is used, pound it and place it between the mixture of butter, sugar and egg; then add the milk, and the flour last. If soda and cream tartar is used, mix the cream tartar with the flour. This mixture is not perfect without the ammonia. Bake in a brisk oven.

## DOUGHNUTS.

Three and one-half pounds of flour, one-half ounce of soda, three-fourths of and ounce of cream tartar, four eggs, one quart of milk, one pound of sugar and three ounces of butter; flavor with nutmeg. Mix the butter and sugar together, then add the eggs, nutmeg, milk, soda and flour. Cut with small cutters, and fry in hot lard.

## NEW YORK GINGER BREAD.

Four pounds of sugar, two and one-half pounds of butter, three pints of eggs, two quarts of milk, one ounce of saleratus, two ounces cream tartar, eight pounds flour and three ounces of yellow ginger. Rub the sugar and butter together as for cake, add the eggs by degrees, mix the cream tartar with the flour, and the saleratus and ginger into the milk. Put the milk into the butter and and eggs, adding the flour last. Put into deep pans and bake in a medium hot oven.

Any of these large recipes can be reduced to as small a quantity as desired. Mr. ED. LEWIS.

## RICH CAKE. No. 1.

Four pounds of sugar, four pounds of butter, two quarts of eggs, four pounds and eight ounces of flour, two ounces of soda and four ounces of cream tartar. Rub the sugar and butter together, add the eggs by degress and the flour last. Bake in medium oven.

## RICH CAKE. No. 2.

Three pounds of sugar, two pounds of butter, three pints of eggs, three gills of milk, one-half ounce of soda, one ounce of cream tartar and two and one-half pounds of flour. Put together as in No. 1.

## RICH CAKE. No. 3.

Three pounds of sugar, one and one-half pounds of butter, one quart of eggs, one quart of milk, one-half ounce of soda, one ounce of cream tartar and three pounds of flour. Mix as No. 1, and bake in deep pans.

## MOLASSES SQUARES.

Two quarts of molasses, one quart of sweet milk, one and one-half pounds of lard, one pound of brown sugar, four ounces of soda and eight ounces of cream tartar. Rub the sugar and lard together, then add the molasses. Dissolve the soda in the milk and add to it. Mix the cream tartar with the dry flour; add enough flour to stiffen so that it can be rolled, and put on buttered sheet pans. Cut in squares, wash over the top with yolk of egg and cream, and bake in a medium hot oven. Mr. ED. LEWIS.

## SUGAR SQUARES.

Three pounds of sugar, two quarts of milk, one and one-half pounds of lard, one ounce of ammonia and one ounce of soda. Mix the sugar and lard well together, pound the ammonia very fine and add; mix the soda in the milk and add to the other ingredients; put in flour enough to stiffen, roll, and cut into squares, put into pans, and do as for molasses squares.

## MACAROON CAKES.

One pound of almond paste, one and one-half pounds of sugar, the whites of eight or nine eggs. Rub the almond and sugar together, work in the whites of the eggs gradually; then drop from hand or spoon in small cakes and bake in a medium oven.

## VANILLA CAKES.

Ten pounds of sugar, six pounds of lard, one quart of eggs, five quarts of milk, four ounces of soda, six ounces of cream tartar, fifteen pounds of flour; salt and mace. Rub the sugar and lard together, adding the eggs by degrees, dissolve the soda in the milk and add, put in the mace also; mix the salt and cream tartar with the dry flour. After being well mixed together, drop from the hand in small cakes and bake in a medium oven. Flavor with vanilla.

## CREAM SHELLS. For Cream Cakes.

Two quarts of water, one and one-fourth pounds of lard, two and one-fourth pounds of flour, salt; two quarts of eggs and one-half ounce of ammonia. Let the water and lard come to a boil; while boiling add the flour and salt; remove from the fire and add one-half of the eggs and ammonia; then put it back again for about three minutes, stirring constantly; then pour out on a large board or wide pan and with a knife, cut it across one way and then the other; add the rest of the eggs and mix well. When cold enough to put the hand in, drop small pieces, about the size of an egg, on a greased flat pan, far apart, so as not to touch; bake in a quick oven, when baked, fill with cream.

## ROCK CAKE.

Three pounds of sugar, three-fourths of a pound of lard, one quart of sour milk, four eggs, one ounce of soda, one ounce of ammonia, salt and lemon. Rub the sugar and lard together, add pounded ammonia, then the eggs. Dissolve the soda in the milk and add the salt and lemon. Flour to stiffen, drop into greased pan and bake in a quick oven.

## DARK FRUIT CAKE. No. 1.

One quart of molasses, three pounds of sugar, two pounds of butter, one and one-half pints of milk, one pint of eggs, seven pounds of currants, four pounds of raisins, one pound of citron, seven and one-half pounds of flour, a little oil of lemon and one-half ounce of soda. Rub together the butter and sugar, put in the eggs by degrees, and a little spice, then add the molasses, soda and milk, flour and the fruit last. Be sure you have the fruit dry. Mix a little flour with the fruit, but rub it all out through a sieve, then add to the other ingredients.

## DARK FRUIT CAKE. No. 2.

Two pounds of sugar, two pounds of butter, three pints of milk, three pints of molasses, nine pounds of flour, one quart of eggs, one ounce of soda, three pounds of citron, six pounds of currants, four pounds of raisins. Mix the same as fruit cake No. 1, and bake in a medium cold oven.

## WEDDING CAKE.

Three pounds of sugar, three pounds of butter, thirty eggs, two ounces of all kinds of spice, one pint of molasses, three pounds and two ounces of flour, four pounds of raisins, two pounds of citron and a little pinch of soda. Rub the butter and sugar well together, add the eggs by degrees, then the molasses, flour and fruit and bake in a medium hot oven.

## POUND CAKE.

One pound of butter, one pound of sugar, twelve eggs, a pinch of mace and one pound and two ounces of flour.    Rub the butter and sugar well together and add the eggs by degrees, then the mace, and the flour last, and bake in a slow oven.

## ANGEL CAKE.

The whites of eleven eggs, nine and one-fourth ounces of sugar, one teaspoonful of cream tartar, five and one-fourth ounces of flour, one teaspoonful of cream tartar sifted with the flour and one teaspoonful of vanilla.    Beat the whites to a stiff froth and add the sugar, then mix in the flour and vanilla ; grease deep pans and fit paper inside, put in the mixture and bake in a slow oven.

# GENERAL REMARKS ON PASTRY.

## GREEN APPLE PIE. No. 1.

Pare, core and quarter twelve green apples; cover the pie-plate with a nice rim paste and place the apples in as level as possible, grate a little nutmeg over the top and put in sugar enough to sweeten ; when cooked cover with another crust, somewhat richer than the bottom paste; put it into a medium hot oven and bake until the apples are cooked ; then, if desired, brush the top of the pie with a little sweet cream to give it a golden brown color.

## GREEN APPLE PIE. No. 2.

Pare, core and cut in squares, twelve apples ; put them on the stove, with a little water, and cover with brown sugar.    Cover the plates as mentioned in No. 1 ; put in the stewed apples, cover and bake.

## APPLE PIE. No. 3.

Stew evaporated apples, and add sugar to sweeten, and the juice of one lemon.    Cover the pie-plates and put in the stewed apples, grate a little nutmeg over the top, cover and bake.

## APPLE PIE. No. 4.

Put some cooked apples into pie-plates, as in Nos. 1 and 2 ; season with a little mace, nutmeg and the juice of one lemon, cover and bake.

## APPLE PIE WITH MERANGUE.

Pare and core apples and make as in No. 1, only have the paste very rich.    Cover the pie-plate with paste a little thicker than ordinary pie-crust; fill with the green apples, season with spice and sweeten to taste ; put in the oven and bake.    Be sure and do not put on the top crust.    After it is cooked, cover with merangue ; put in the oven and brown.    Serve when cold.

## BLUEBERRY PIE.

Make a paste as for apple pies, fill with nice blueberries and grate a little cinnamon over them, cover with sugar and sprinkle in a little flour to hold them together, cover with pie-crust and bake.

## RASPBERRY PIE.

Cover pie-plates as for blueberry pie; fill with raspberries, add sugar and a little flour to hold them together, cover with pie-crust and bake.

## HUCKLEBERRY PIE.

Make and season the same as blueberries.

## PEACH PIE. No. 1.

Cover pie-plates with paste; fill with canned peaches and grate a little nutmeg or cinnamon over the top, cover with sugar, put on the top crust and bake.

## PEACH PIE. No. 2.

Cover pie-plate with paste; pare, and remove the stones from uncooked peaches, arrange on a plate and grate over them a little nutmeg or cinnamon, cover with sugar; cut pie paste in long strips and cover across one way and then arrange three or four strips across the other; put into the oven and bake.

## APPLE POT-PIE.

Fourteen apples, peeled. cored and sliced, one and one-half pints of flour, one teaspoonful of Royal baking powder, one cup of sugar, one-half a cup of butter, one cup of milk and a large pinch of salt. Sift the flour, powder and salt together, rub in the butter cold and add the milk. Mix into dough as for tea biscuit, with it line a shallow stew-pan to within two inches of the bottom, pour in the apples, sugar and one and one-half cupsful of water, wet the sides and cover with the rest of the dough, boil twenty minutes, then place in the oven to cook the apples; remove from the oven, cut the top crust into four equal parts, dish the apples and lay on them pieces of the side crust cut in diamonds, and pieces of the top crust.

## BLACKBERRY PIE.

One-half cup of sugar, three cups of berries to each pie; line the pieplates with paste, put in the berries and sugar, moisten the edges, cover and wash with milk; bake in a quick, steady oven twenty minutes.

## CRANBERRY PIE.

Stew three cups of cranberries with one and one-half cups of sugar and strain; line the pie-plate with paste, fill with the cranberry jam; wash the edges, lay three bars across, fasten the edges, then place three more, forming diamond shaped spaces, lay rim of paste, brush with egg and bake in a quick oven until the paste is cooked.

## CUSTARD PIE.

Four eggs, one cup of sugar, one tablespoonful of extract of lemon; line a well greased pie-plate with paste one fourth of an inch thick. Take a ball of paste, flour it well, and with the palm of the left hand proceed to press against the edges, pushing the paste from the centre into a thick, high rim on the edge of the plate, fill while in the oven with the sugar, milk, eggs and extract beaten together.

## COCOANUT PIE.

Proceed as for plain custard pie; add one and one-half cups of cocoanut, and leave out one-half pint of milk.

## CHERRY PIE.

Three cups of steamed cherries and one cup of sugar; line the pie-plate with paste, wet the edges and add the cherries, cover and bake in a steady oven.

## APPLE CUSTARD PIE.

Proceed as for custard pie, adding thickly stewed apples.

## PEACH CUSTARD PIE.

Proceed as for custard pie, laying in the bottom some cooked or canned peaches and placing the custard over them.

## CURRANT PIE.

Stew three cups of ripe currants with one cup of sugar ten minutes, strain and make as you would cranberry pie,

## PLUM PIE.

Two cups of prunes steeped in water over night, one cup of sugar and one tablespoonful of extract of lemon. Line the pie-plate with paste, wet the edges, add the prunes with the sugar, one-third cup of water and the extract; cover, wash with milk and bake in a hot oven twenty minutes.

## GOOSEBERRY PIE.

Three cups of gooseberries stewed with one and one-half cups of sugar fifteen or twenty minutes, strain and make as you would cranberry pie.

## LEMON CREAM PIE.

One and one-half pints of milk, three tablespoonsful of cornstarch, one cup of sugar, two tablespoonsful of butter, one tablespoonful of extract of lemon; cloves, cinnamon, the juice of two lemons and the yolks of four eggs. Boil the milk and add the cornstarch dissolved in a little milk; when this boils beat in the yolks, lemon juice, extract and butter and pour at once into the pie-plate, lined with paste, having a high rim as described for cocoanut or custard pie. Bake in a hot oven until the paste is cooked.

## LEMON CREAM PIE WITH MERANGUE.

Having made the lemon cream pie, whip the whites of four eggs to a dry froth, slowly adding one cup of sugar; spread over the top of the pie and return to the oven to brown slightly.

## LEMON PIE.

Two soda crackers, two lemons, one and one-half cups of coffee sugar, two eggs and one and one-half cups of boiling water. Roll the crackers fine and pour on the boiling water, cover with a plate, and when cold, add the beaten eggs, sugar, the grated rind of one and the juice of two lemons; line the pie-plate with paste, add the ingredients, wet the edges, cover, wash with milk and bake in a quick oven twenty minutes.

## ORANGE PIE.

Four eggs, two tablespoonsful of butter, one-half pint of cream, one cup of sugar, the juice of two oranges and the rind of one. Beat the butter and sugar to a light cream, add the beaten eggs gradually, with the juice and grated rind last; add the cream whipped to a stiff froth. Line the pie-plate with paste, wash the edges, put on rims and pour in the mixture; bake in a slow oven twenty minutes.

## MINCE MEAT. No. 1.

Seven pounds of currants, three and one-half pounds of peeled and cored apples, three and one-half pounds of beef, three and one-half pounds of suet, one-half pound each of citron, lemon and orange peel, two and one-half pounds of sugar, two pounds of raisins, four nutmegs, one ounce of cinnamon, one-half ounce each of cloves and mace, one pint brandy and one pint of white wine.

Wash the currants dry and pick them, stone the raisins, remove the skin and sinews from the beef and suet; chop each ingredient separate very fine, put them into a large pan as they are finished, finally adding the spices, brandy and wine thoroughly mixed together; pack into jars and store in a cold, dry place. This mince meat will keep from twelve to eighteen months. Fruit should never be floured for mince meat.

## MINCE MEAT. No. 2.

Two pounds of currants, five pounds of peeled and cored apples, two pounds of lean, boiled beef, one pound of beef suet, three-fourths of a pound of citron, two and one-pounds of sugar, two pounds of raisins, one pound of seedless raisins, two table-sponsful of cinnamon, one nutmeg, one tablespoonful each of mace, cloves and allspice and one pint each of Maderia wine and brandy.

Wash the currants dry and pick them, stone the raisins, remove the skin and sinews from the beef; chop each ingredient very fine, separate; place as soon as done in a large pan and finally add spice, wine and brandy; mix thoroughly, pack in jars and keep in a cool place.

## MINCE MEAT. No. 3.

Two pounds of currants, two pounds of beef suet, one pound of raisins, one and one-half pounds of sugar, four ounces candied orange peel, one half pint each of red and white wine, very thin peel of two lemons and one teaspoonful each of cinnamon, cloves and nutmeg.

Wash the currants, stone the raisins and free the suet of skin. Chop each ingredient separately very fine; as soon as done place into pans, finally adding the spices and wines; mix thoroughly, pack into jars and store in a cool place. Line the pie-plates with paste, wet the edges, put in the mince meat, cover, wash over with egg and bake in a quick oven.

## HOW TO DISTRIBUTE RAISINS IN A MINCE PIE.

When the mince meat is ready for the crust, prepare the raisins and put them into a basin on the stove, with sufficient water to cover them; cook until tender; after you have filled the crust, you can put in the raisins so that about the same number will come in each piece, then if you wet the edges of the crust so that the juice will not escape, you cannot tell by the taste that the raisins were not cooked with the minced meat.

## PLUM PIE.

Let three cups of plums simmer in water, covered with one and one-half cups of sugar, until tender; line the pie-plate with paste, wet the edges, cover, wash with egg and bake in a quick oven.

## PUMPKIN PIE.

Wash and boil one large sized pumpkin, just as you would potatoes with the skins on; when thoroughly cooked pass through a sieve, cleaning it free from all lumps, seeds, etc. Take one cup of sugar and one cup of molasses mixed well together, thoroughly beat four eggs and mix with the pumpkin; then add the molasses and sugar, a pinch of salt, four teaspoonsful of ginger, one teaspoonful of cinnamon and one cup of milk; mix well together. This is intended to make from five to six pies. Should the pumpkin not be a large one, add less milk. Bake in deep plates lined with firm paste.

## SQUASH PIE.

Make the same as pumpkin pie.

## RICE PIE.

One-half a cup of rice, one half a pint of milk, one-half a pint of cream, three eggs, a pinch of salt and one cup of sugar. Boil the rice in one-half a pint of water till very soft, add the milk and run through the sieve, then add the cream, beaten egg, salt and sugar. Line the plate as for custard pie and pour in the mixture and bake in a hot oven about twenty minutes.

## RHUBARB PIE.

One and one-half bunches of rhubarb, one and one-half cups of sugar. Cut in small pieces after the skin is removed, cook very fast in a shallow pan with the sugar; line the pie-plate with paste, wet the rim and add the rhubarb cold. Lay three bars of the paste across the top, fastening the ends, lay three more across, forming diamond shaped spaces; put on a rim, wash over with egg and bake in a quick oven twenty minutes.

## STRAWBERRY PIE.

Proceed as directed for Raspberry pie.

## SOUTHERN MINCE PIE.

Six apples, half the quantity of raisins, one-half a pound of suet. Remove the skin from the suet, stone the raisins, chop the apples separate from the other ingredients. Mix together and chop them very fine, adding two cups of black molasses, the same of brown sugar, two nutmegs, the same of cinnamon, a few blades of mace and one cup of brandy; cook slowly for one hour; after it is cold, line the pie-plates with paste, fill, and bake in a quick oven twenty minutes.

## PIE PASTE. Plain.

One pound of flour, one-half pound of butter; rub the butter and dry flour well together, make a hole in the centre and pour in cold water, mixing it quite stiff.

## PASTE. No. 2.

One pound of flour and one-fourth of a pound of butter; rub together as for paste No. 1.

## MEDIUM RICH PASTE.

One pound of flour and three-fourths of a pound of butter; rub the butter with the dry flour, make a hole in the centre and add one half water and one-half milk; mix quite stiff.

BARBERRIES.

CRANBERRIES.

STRAWBERRIES.

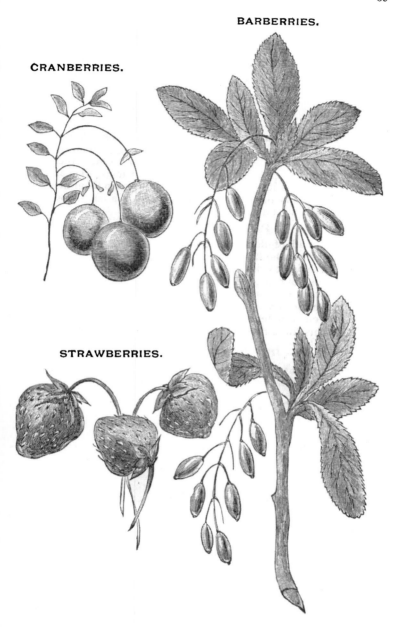

## PUFF PASTE. No. 1.

One pound of flour and three-quarters of a pound of butter; take a piece of butter, about the size of an egg, and rub dry with the flour, mix with a little cold water very stiff and roll out somewhat square, thin at the ends and thick in the centre; have the butter well washed, but stiff and hard so that it will not run, make into a flat, square cake and put in the centre of the paste, then cover by folding the four corners over the top; with a heavy rolling-pin flatten it to fasten the ends together, then roll out square; put it into a cool place and let it stand fifteen minutes so that the paste will get firm; take out and roll out long, letting the ends be square, fold half way, then fold the other end over to meet the outside; dust with flour and roll the opposite side the same. Be careful and not let the paste stick to the pin or table but keep them well dusted with flour. This paste should be worked in a cool room so that the butter will not melt.

## PUFF PASTE. No. 2.

One pound of flour and one-half pound of butter; wash out all the salt from the butter in ice water; have it free from the milk and water, have it firm and solid, take a small piece of it and rub dry with the flour, mix the flour with cold water till quite stiff, roll out, then break the butter into small pieces and cover the centre allowing the four ends to cover it, roll with a pin and place in a cool place for ten minutes; dust with flour, then roll and fold as paste No. 1, do this three times, then it is ready for use.

### RIM PASTE. Very plain.

One pound of flour and two ounces of butter; rub the butter and flour together, mix with cold water, very stiff, roll out and line pie plates.

### RICH PASTE FOR MEAT PIES.

One pound of flour and one pound of butter; mix as other pastes mentioned and roll out thick.

### MEDIUM PASTE FOR MEAT PIES.

One pound of flour, one-half pound of butter and one tablespoonful of baking powder; mix the butter and flour together dry, add the powder, mix with water and roll out thick.

# PUDDINGS.

There are many ways of making puddings, both rich and plain. Many times we have pieces of bread and cake that would be burnt or thrown into the crumb basket, which an economical cook would know what to do with. A housekeeper buys many times when it is not needed, by not knowing what could be utilized to make a good and palatable pudding.

To be good, experienced housekeepers and cooks we must use everything that can be used in the line of cooking, such as odds and ends that are left and that can be prepared again for the dinner table, in another shape and style. So you see what we can do by being economical and trying to save. An extravagant housekeeper makes an extravagant cook, because she wants everything that is in the market and brings it to the cook, and if the cook cannot find a use for it, it goes into the waste pails. An economical housekeeper will oftentimes make the cook and others about the house saving; but when the housekeeper does not care, why should the cook? because it does not cost him or her anything but the trouble to get it out of the way and call for more.

GEORGE F. BRAXTON, Chef.

### BREAD PUDDING. Plain.

Take pieces of bread, left from breakfast or dinner, butter one side of each slice, put into a dish; scald milk enough to cover the bread, when poured over allow a little more than will cover, because the bread will soak it all up; sweeten the milk with brown sugar and flavor it with a little nutmeg or cinnamon, when well scalded pour over the bread; after the bread has soaked it up pour on a little more, just enough to cover it, bake in a medium hot oven and serve with plain beaten cream.

### BREAD PUDDING. No. 1.

Take pieces of bread, break in small pieces, put some in the bottom of a dish, then put small pieces of butter on top, then a few raisins, put on another layer of bread crumbs, then apply butter and raisins as before; when the dish is nearly full take as much milk as will cover the bread; add a few beaten eggs to the milk to form a custard, grate in a little nutmeg, mix the eggs and milk well together, add sugar to sweeten, run through a hair sieve, pour over the bread, put into the oven, bake and serve with beaten sweet cream.

### ENGLISH BREAD PUDDING. Very nice.

Soak pieces of bread in cold milk. Use stoned raisins, chopped, and currants; beat six eggs and add to milk, to moisten, grate in a little nutmeg and cloves, one teaspoonful of cinnamon and sugar to sweeten. Strain the milk and eggs. After the eggs and other ingredients are mixed in the milk, pour it on the moistened bread, add currants and raisins, mix it well almost as you would cake, put in covered tin pans, steam or boil about four hours and serve with hard sauce.

### QUEEN'S PUDDING.

Make as bread pudding No. 1. After it is cooked, cover with raspberry jam or cider jelly, beat whites of eggs to a froth, cover, put in the oven and let brown and serve with cream sauce.

## TROY PUDDING.

Soak pieces of bread in milk. Mix the bread fine to a pulp, add a little flour to hold together, add one cupful of molasses, two of sugar, put chopped, stoned raisins and currants into milk, mix the bread and flour, add twelve eggs, two nutmegs, two cloves, one teaspoonful of cinnamon and two tablespoonsful of baking powder; mix it with a little butter, put the mixture in deep, greased pans, cover and steam from three to four hours. Serve with lemon sauce.

## PLUM PUDDING. No. 1.

Two pounds of flour, one pound of beef suet, two table-spoonsful of lemon extract, four pounds of raisins, four pounds of currants, a little allspice, nutmeg and clove to flavor, one gill of molasses, one gill of brown sugar, one gill of brandy, sixteen eggs, one pound of citron, orange and lemon peel, one cup of milk and two teaspoonsful of baking powder into the flour. Chop the suet very fine, chop the orange and lemon peel and citron, stone and chop the raisins, chop the currants, wash and dry. Put beef suet, currants, raisins, citron, lemon and orange peel, spices, milk and molasses into a bowl, with the eggs last, carefully mixed together; sift the flour with the baking powder and mix with the other ingredients, put in deep pans, cover and steam from four to four and one-half hours. After it is cooked, turn out on a dish carefully, stick almonds around it and serve with hard or brandy sauce.

## PLUM PUDDING. No. 2.

One and one-half cupsful of bread crumbs, suet chopped very fine, raisins, seeded currants, washed and picked, coffee sugar, one-half cupful each of citron, milk, and orange marmalade; four eggs, two cupsful of flour, one teaspoonful of baking powder, one teaspoonful of extract of cinnamon, cloves and nutmeg; mix these ingredients well together in a large bowl; then put in well-buttered moulds, set in a sauce-pan of boiling water that will reach half way up its sides, steam two and one-half hours, turn out on a dish and serve with hard sauce.

## PLUM PUDDING. No. 3.

One and one-half cupsful of finely chopped suet, two cupsful of seeded raisins, one cupful of currants, washed and picked, one-half a cupful of sugar, one-half a cupful of chopped citron, one glass of white wine, two and one-half cupsful of flour, one teaspoonful of baking powder, one cupful of milk, one teaspoonful of extract, nutmeg and lemon; place all these ingredients in a bowl with beaten eggs, flour sifted with the powder; mix into a firm batter, put into well buttered moulds, set in a sauce-pan of boiling water, boil two and one-half hours, turn out and serve with hard sauce.

## PLUM PUDDING. No. 4.

Two cupsful each of stoned raisins, currants, washed and picked, beef suet chopped fine, granulated sugar, three cupsful of grated bread crumbs, eight eggs, one cupful each of citron and almonds (blanched by putting water on them until the skins slip off easily), lemon peel and a large pinch of salt. Mix all these ingredients together in a large bowl; put in well buttered moulds, set in a sauce-pan of boiling water and steam about five hours. When cooked, turn out carefully and serve with brandy or wine sauce.

## FRENCH PLUM PUDDING.

One-half pound of beef kidney grease, one-half pound of raisins (Smyrna and Malaga mixed), one-half pound of fresh bread crumbs, one tablespoonful of flour, six ounces of powdered sugar, four ounces of orange peel and citron mixed, a little salt, one fourth of a grated nutmeg, a pinch of pulverized ginger, a little chopped lemon peel, five eggs, two tablespoonsful of good brandy and one-half a tablespoonful of sweet cream. This is sufficient for a good sized pudding. Wash the raisins in luke-warm water and put them in a bowl with the peel already cut in square pieces, and steep in a little brandy; now turn on the beef kidney fat and chop very fine, with a spoonful of flour, mix it well with the crumbs of bread, brown sugar and eggs, then add the raisins, peel, the rest of the brandy, salt, nutmeg, ginger and last of all, and after it is well mixed, the cream; spread all this in a large, well buttered napkin, fold up the corners and tie to the level of the pudding so as to make it round; then plunge it into a sauce-pan of boiling water and boil constantly four hours; take it out and let drain in a seive, cut it from the top so as to keep it level, turn it out on a dish and remove the napkin carefully so as not to disturb the fine part of the pudding; sprinkle with a little rum sauce. You may apply a match to the pudding when it is on the table. Serve with a little brandy sauce separate. This pudding may be cooked in a mould, the mould well buttered and the pudding tied in a napkin, also well buttered.

## RICE PUDDING. No. 1.

One-half a cupful of rice, one-half pint of milk, one-half cup of sugar, a large pinch of salt and one tablespoonful of lemon rind chopped fine. Put rice, washed and picked, sugar, salt and milk in a quart pudding dish; bake in a moderate oven two hours, permit it to finish cooking with light colored crust, disturbing it no more. Eat cold with cream.

## RICE PUDDING. No. 2.

One cupful of rice, one quart of milk, four eggs, one tablespoonful of butter, one cup of sugar and a pinch of salt. Boil the rice in one pint of milk until tender, then remove from the fire; add eggs, sugar, salt and milk, beaten together; pour into pudding dish, break the butter into small pieces on the surface. Bake in steady oven ten minutes and serve with brandy sauce.

## RICE PUDDING. No. 3.

One-half a cupful of rice, one-fourth pint of milk, four apples, peeled, cored and stewed, one-third cupful of sugar and four eggs. Boil the rice in milk until reduced to pulp, beat well with apple sauce and sugar for ten minutes and set aside to cool; then carefully mix in whites of eggs, whipped to a stiff froth, pour the pudding into buttered moulds, set in a sauce-pan of boiling water reaching half-way up the sides; steam slowly about twenty-five minutes, permit to stand about three minutes before turning out and serve with custard sauce.

## TAPIOCA PUDDING.

One cupful of tapioca soaked in three cups of cold water over night, one and one-half cups of sugar, one pint of milk and five eggs; proceed as for rice pudding No. 2.

## SAGO PUDDING.

One pint of milk, four tablespoonsful of sago boiled in the milk until soft; set the dish in a kettle of hot water and let the sago swell gradually. Stir four beaten eggs into the cooked milk and sago, salt and sweeten to taste, put into the oven and bake very lightly. Sauce:—two-thirds of a cupful of butter, beaten to a cream, stir in sugar until quite thick, and two cupsful of boiling water; add cornstarch mixed with cold water until the whole is of the consistency of thin starch; mix this with sugar and butter; pour one-half over pudding while boiling hot, and the other half just before serving, after adding one teaspoonful of extract of vanilla or lemon to give it a rich flavor.

## SWEET POTATO PUDDING.

Six good sized potatoes grated raw, one tablespoonful of butter, one tablespoonful of lard, one pint of molasses, three tablespoonsful of brown sugar, one-half pint of milk, one egg, one teaspoonful each of cloves, allspice and ginger, two teaspoonsful of salt and water to make a soft batter. Stir two or three times while baking. Bake slowly two hours.

## POOR MAN'S PUDDING.

One-half cupful of chopped suet, one-half cupful of seeded raisins, one-half cupful of currants, washed and picked, one and one-half cupsful of bread crumbs, one cupful of flour, one table-spoonful of baking powder, one-half cupful of brown sugar and one pint of milk.   Mix all well together, put into a well greased mould, set in sauce-pan of boiling water, reaching half-way up the sides; steam two hours, turn out on a dish carefully and serve with butter and sugar.

## PRINCESS PUDDING.

Two-thirds of a cup of butter, one cup of sugar, one large cup or flour, three eggs, one-half teaspoonful of baking powder and a small glass of brandy.   Rub butter and sugar to a smooth cream, add eggs one at a time, beating a few minutes between; add flour, sifted with powder, and brandy.   Put into moulds well buttered, set into a sauce-pan of hot water, reaching half-way up the sides; steam one and one half hours, turn out on dish carefully and serve with lemon sauce.

## PROFESSOR THORNTON'S PUDDING.

Three cups of bread crumbs, one-half cup of currants, one-half cup each of chopped citron, orange peel and lemon peel, one-half cup of sugar, three eggs, one pint of milk and one tablespoon-ful of butter.   Grate the bread into a bowl and pour over the boiling milk; cover with a plate twenty minutes, then add the beaten eggs, sugar, citron, lemon and orange peel, melted butter and currants, well washed and picked; mix and fill six well greased cups.   Bake in a quick oven twenty-five minutes.   When about to serve turn out on a platter and pour around it wine sauce.

## CRACKER AND JAM PUDDING.

Three eggs, one-half cupful of cracker crumbs, one-half cup-ful of sugar, one tablespoonful of butter, one cup of milk, the juice of one half a lemon with grated peel and three tablespoonsful of jam.   Heat the milk and crumbs together till scalded, turn out to cool.   Rub butter and sugar to a cream adding the lemon, stir in the beaten yolks of the eggs, the soaked cracker and milk, and put the whites in last; put the jam at the bottom, and fill up with the mixture.   Bake covered one-half an hour, then brown.   Eat cold with powdered sugar sprinkled over the top, or, if you like, put a merangue over the top.

## COTTAGE PUDDING.  No. 1.

One cup of sugar, two cups of cream, two eggs, one pint of flour and one and one-half tablespoonsful of baking powder.   Beat the eggs and sugar together; add cream, flour with baking-powder sifted into it and a pinch of salt.   Mix into a smooth batter as for cup cake, put into long, narrow or oval buttered moulds.   Bake in a hot oven thirty minutes.

## COTTAGE PUDDING. No. 2.

One cup of sugar, one cup of milk, one egg, a lump of butter the size of an egg, one pint of flour, salt and two tablespoonsful of baking powder. Bake in a quick oven.

## CUSTARD PUDDING.

One and one half pints of milk, four eggs, one cup of sugar, two tablespoonsful of extract of vanilla. Beat eggs and sugar together, dilute with milk and extract; pour into buttered pudding dish, set in the oven in a dripping pan two-thirds full of boiling water. Bake in a moderate oven about forty minutes.

## ARROW-ROOT PUDDING.

One quart of milk, three and one-half tablespoonsful of arrowroot, four eggs, one cup of sugar and one tablespoonful of extract of nutmeg and cinnamon. Boil the milk, add arrowroot dissolved in a little water and sugar. Take it from the fire and beat in the eggs, whipped a little, and the extract; pour in a well buttered earthern dish and bake in a quick oven one-half hour. A few minutes before taking from the oven sift two tablespoonsful of sugar over it and set it back to glaze. Eat cold.

## CORN STARCH PUDDING.

Proceed as for arrow-root pudding.

## CHOCOLATE PUDDING.

One pint of scalded cream, one and one-half squares of Baker's German chocolate, grated and wet with cold milk; stir this into the scalded milk; when the chocolate is dissolved pour it into a pudding dish. Add the yolks of six well beaten eggs and six tablespoonsful of sugar; bake about three quarters of an hour; beat the whites of the eggs to a stiff froth, add six tablespoonsful of sugar, spread the froth over the top and set in the oven again to brown slightly. Eat with sweet cream or milk.

## FIG PUDDING.

One-half pound of good, dried figs, washed, wiped and minced; two cups of fine, dried bread crumbs, three eggs, one-half cup of beef suet, powdered; two scant cups of sweet milk, one-half cup of white sugar, a little salt and one half teaspoonful of baking powder dissolved in hot water and stirred into the milk. Soak the crumbs in the milk; add the eggs, beaten lightly, with sugar, salt, suet and figs; beat three minutes, put into buttered moulds with tight top, set in boiling water with weight on top and boil three hours. Eat hot with hard sauce.

## FARINA PUDDING.

Proceed as for arrow-root pudding.

## GERMAN PUDDING.

Three large potatoes, a pinch of salt, one cup of suet, one-half cup of coffee sugar, one egg, one half tablespoonful of baking powder and one-half cup of cream.    Peel, boil and mash the potatoes very fine ; add eggs, cream, sugar and salt; when cold, add suet and flour sifted with the powder.    Bake in buttered pudding dishes thirty minutes in a quick oven.    Serve with wine sauce.

## HOMINY PUDDING.

Two-thirds of a cup of hominy, one and one half pints of milk, two eggs, one tablespoonful of butter, one tablespoonful of extract of rose and one cup of sugar.    Boil the hominy in milk one hour, then pour it on the eggs, extract and sugar beaten together; add butter.    Pour in buttered pudding dish and bake twenty minutes in a hot oven.

## HUCKLEBERRY PUDDING.

Three sugar muffins or bread, three tablespoonsful of huckleberries, one cup of sugar, one teaspoonful each of extract of cinnamon and cloves, one and one-half pints of milk, three eggs and a pinch of salt.    Grate the muffins and place in a bowl ; pour over the boiling milk, cover with a plate and let it stand thirty minutes. Add eggs, sugar, salt, extract and berries ; mix and put into buttered pudding dishes and bake forty-five minutes.    Serve with wine sauce.

## BAKED INDIAN PUDDING. No. 1.

Three corn muffins or bread, one and one-half pints of milk, one half cup of sugar, three eggs, one tablespoonful each of extract of ginger and cinnamon and one pinch of salt.    Steep the muffins in milk ; when soaked, squeeze rather dry and place in a bowl ; beat up with the sugar, salt, eggs and extract; pour the boiling milk over them, stirring all the time.    Pour in buttered pudding dish and bake one hour in a moderate oven.    Serve with liquid sauce.

## BAKED INDIAN PUDDING. No. 2.

One-half cup of flour, one and one-half cups of corn meal, one-half cup of syrup, one-half teaspoonful of salt and one quart of milk, Mix the flour, corn meal, salt and a cup of milk together, pour the rest on it boiling ; stir once in a while for thirty minutes.    Bake in a moderate oven two hours.    Serve with wine sauce.

## LEMON PUDDING.

Four muffins, or stale bread, the juice of two lemons, one tablespoonful of extract of lemon, one cup of sugar, four eggs, one tablespoonful of butter and one pint of milk.    Grate the muffins, and put into a bowl ; pour the boiling milk over it, cover with a plate and set aside for thirty minutes ; then add sugar, butter, beaten eggs, extract and lemon juice mixed together.    Pour in buttered pudding dish and bake in a hot oven thirty minutes.    Serve with lemon sauce.

## LEMON SUET PUDDING. Very nice.

Four muffins, or stale bread, one cup of suet, one-half cup of sugar, four eggs, one tablespoonful of extract of lemon, one and one-half pints of milk and a pinch of salt. Chop the suet, freed from skin, very fine; grate the muffins and put them into a bowl; add sugar, beaten eggs, salt and extract, pour over the boiling milk, stirring it all the while; let it stand covered thirty minutes. Pour into well buttered pudding dish and bake in a moderate oven forty minutes. Serve with sweet sauce.

## MACARONI PUDDING.

Two cups of broken Italian macaroni, two and one-half pints of milk, two cups of sugar, two large tablespoonsful of butter and two teaspoonsful extract of vanilla. Boil the macaroni fifteen minutes in well salted water, add the boiling milk and let simmer twenty minutes longer. Remove from the fire and pour in the sugar, eggs and butter beaten together; add the extract last. Pour into well buttered pudding dish and bake in a steady oven thirty minutes. Serve with cream sauce.

## MERINGUE RICE PUDDING.

Take two cups of rice to one quart of water. When the rice is boiled dry, add one quart of milk, a piece of butter the size of two eggs, the beaten yolks of eight eggs and the grated rind of one lemon; mix with the rice. Pour the mixture in a buttered dish and bake lightly. Beat the whites of the eggs to a stiff froth, add a cup of sugar and the juice of one lemon. When the pudding is nearly done, spread on the frosting. Bake in a slow oven until the top is a light brown.

## BRISTOL PUDDING.

One quart of sifted flour, three pints of milk, two gills of rich cream, twelve apples, eight eggs and two salt spoonsful of salt. Pare the apples, and core without cutting. Mix the batter very smoothly and pour over the apples. Bake one hour. Serve with lemon sauce.

## APPLE DUMPLINGS. No. 1.

Six apples, peeled, cored and sliced; one cup of sugar. Line six well greased cups with the paste, rolled thin; wet the edges, fill with apples, put in some of the sugar; cover with more paste. Put in shallow stew-pan, large enough to contain them, with boiling water to reach half way up the sides of the cups. Steam forty minutes. Turn out on dish and sprinkle powdered sugar over them. Serve with spice or lemon sauce.

## APPLE DUMPLINGS. No. 2.

Six apples, peeled, cored and sliced; one cup of sugar. Make paste and roll thin, almost square; fill the paste with apples and sprinkle with sugar. Roll the paste, with the apples inside, turning the paste in at the corners to prevent the apples from falling out. Put in a clean, white cloth, and sew up the ends. Boil one hour in a kettle of boiling water. Serve with wine sauce.

## COMMON BATTER.

Two cups of flour, one teaspoonful of baking powder, a pinch of salt, four eggs and two cups of milk. Sift the flour, salt and baking powder together; add the beaten eggs and milk mixed into a batter as for griddle cakes.

## HUCKLEBERRY DUMPLINGS.

Make as directed for apple dumplings No. 2.

## PEACH DUMPLINGS.

Proceed as for apple dumplings No. 2.

## STRAWBERRY DUMPLINGS.

Make as directed for apple dumplings No. 2.

## FARINA DUMPLINGS.

One quart of milk, ten ounces of farina, three eggs, one and one-half tablespoonsful of baking powder, one tablespoonful of butter and one-half pound of fine flour. Bring the milk to a boil, stir in the farina and boil till well done, stirring constantly. When cool, stir in the melted butter, and eggs, previously beaten; and last add the sifted flour, baking powder and salt. Drop with tablespoon into boiling water, well salted. Boil about fifteen minutes. Take out with skimmer. Serve with fruit sauce.

## SUET DUMPLINGS.

Two cups of suet chopped fine, two cups of grated muffins or bread, two cups of flour, one teaspoonful of baking powder, one cup of sugar, four eggs, one quart of milk and a large pinch of salt. Sift together the flour, powder and salt; add the beaten eggs, grated muffins, sugar, suet and milk. Form into a smooth batter and drop by tablespoonsful into a quart of boiling milk, three or four at a time. When done, dish and pour over them the milk they were boiled in.

## CALVES LIVER DUMPLINGS. Very nice.

A calf's liver well washed, skinned and scraped with a sharp knife, taking out all the stringy parts or sinews; add to this the same quantity of stale wheat bread, grated fine; pepper and salt to taste. Cut onions stewed in a little butter may be added, if liked. Mix well and form into balls; put into boiling water and boil about fifteen minutes. Take out with skimmer. Serve with any kind of meat fricassee.

# DESSERTS AND ICES.

## CHARLOTTE RUSSE.

One-half package of Cox's gelatine, one pint of cream, one-half cup of white wine, four lemons, the whites of five eggs, one tablespoonful of vanilla and one pound of powdered sugar. Soak the gelatine in cold water or milk, just cover it with water and let soak till very soft; then dissolve it on the stove, and strain. Beat the cream to a stiff froth, also the whites of the eggs; add the juice of the lemons and the sugar. Mix the cream and whites together, put the vanilla into the gelatine, and pour the wine and gelatine to the other ingredients, stirring slowly till it thickens. Line moulds with sponge cake; pour in the mixture, and set in a cool place until ready for use.

## CHARLOTTE RUSSE. No. 2.

One-half package of gelatine, one gill of white wine, one pint of cream, the whites of three eggs, two lemons, one teaspoonful of vanilla, three-quarters of a pound of powdered sugar and the yolks of three eggs. Proceed as for charlotte russe No. 1, only beat the yolks separate with sugar and add last. Stir in the gelatine until stiff.

## CHARLOTTE RUSSE. No. 3.

One cup of cream, four lemons, three-quarters of a pound of powdered sugar, the whites of four eggs and one-half teaspoonful of vanilla. Beat the cream very stiff, and the eggs to a froth; add the juice of lemons, and vanilla last; sugar and mix well together. Line moulds with cake, pour in the mixture and let stand until ready for use.

## CHARLOTTE RUSSE. No. 4.

Two tablespoonsful of gelatine soaked in a little cold milk two hours, two cups of rich cream and one teacup of milk. Whip the cream stiff in a large bowl and set on the ice. Boil milk and pour it over the gelatine until it is dissolved, then strain; when cold add whipped cream, a spoonful at a time, sweeten with powdered sugar and flavor with vanilla. Line dish with lady fingers or sponge cake, pour on the mixture and set in a cool place to harden.

Custards require to be made carefully, and need not, unless occasion demands it, be made expensively. The plain, boiled custard, usually served with tarts or puddings, may be cheaply prepared. Custards may have the delicate flavor of lemon, orange, rose, vanilla, nutmeg, etc., communicated to them by flavoring extracts. A few drops of rose will answer where a teaspoonful of vanilla would be required. By their use the necessity of straining the custard is avoided. Flavoring should be used after boiling, that the fine aroma need not be lost by the heat.

## BANANA CUSTARD.

Bake a white custard as follows:—two tablespoonsful of corn starch, wet with enough water to dissolve it, one cup of granulated sugar and one-third cup of butter. Stir together into a pudding mould or earthern dish and pour in enough water to make a thick custard. Beat the whites of three eggs to snow and stir into the custard. Bake fifteen minutes in the oven, or for the same length of time in a pot of boiling water. Set aside until perfectly cold, then remove the slight crust that will have formed on top. Have ready the dish in which you are to serve your custard, and some fresh, ripe bananas, minced finely. Mix with the custard and pour into the dish. Add a meringue made of the beaten whites of eggs and one-half cup of powdered sugar.

A fine custard may be made according to the above recipe by using peaches instead of bananas, or Bartlett pears. Milk should never be used with acid fruits, particularly in warm weather; and pure cream in any quantity is a severe tax on a weak stomach.

The custards for which formulae are given here, can be made thus as real cream, and answer the same purposes, and in most cases are quite as palatable as the ordinary milk cream, and are without the danger of being curdled by the acidity of the fruit.

Tapioca, arrow-root, etc., may be substituted for corn starch in the making of these custards. Pineapples, raspberries and strawberries are delicious served in this way. Custards with an extra allowance of butter and a flavoring of vanilla, almond or rose. make delicious cream pies. Bake with either one or two crusts of rich puff paste. If the former, make a meringue by using the yolks as well as the whites of the eggs.

By using the grated rind and juice of lemons or oranges, or both, delicous orange and lemon pies are made. These should be made with only one crust.

## BANANA PIES.

Make a white custard as above, and mix with the pulp of ripe bananas, pressed through a cullender or sieve. Bake in a rich, open pastry crust and finish with a meringue.

## CHOCOLATE CUSTARD.

Pour two tablespoonsful of boiling water over two ounces of grated chocolate; let it stand near the fire till perfectly dissolved, add a pint of milk mixed with a pint of cream, a pinch of salt and three ounces of sugar. Simmer over the fire ten minutes, then add the yolks of eight beaten eggs and stir to a froth while it thickens. Pour out to cool.

## BOILED CUSTARD.

One quart of milk, eight eggs, the peel of one large lemon, three laurel leaves and one-half pound of sugar. Pour the milk into a sauce-pan with the laurel leaves and lemon peel; set on the stove twenty minutes and when on the point of boiling, strain into a bowl to cool. Stir in the sugar and beaten eggs; again strain into a jug, place in a deep sauce-pan of boiling water and stir one way until it thickens. Pour into custard cups and serve with cider jelly at the bottom.

## VANILLA CUSTARD.

Boil one pint of cream with four ounces of sugar one-quarter of an hour, then strain through muslin. Beat the yolks of six eggs and pour milk over them into a bowl, placing the bowl over a pan of boiling water and stirring rapidly till it thickens. Let it cool gradually; add one teaspoonful of extract of vanilla, and stir continually. When cold, serve in a dish covered with the whipped whites of eggs sifted over with sugar.

## CHOCOLATE BLANC MANGE.

One quart of milk, one-half box of gelatine soaked in a cup of water, four tablespoonsful of grated chocolate rubbed smooth in a little milk, three eggs and extract of vanilla. Heat the milk until it boils, then add the other ingredients. Boil eight minutes and pour into moulds. Serve with cream or custard.

## TARTS.

Currants, gooseberries, apple or other fruits can be used for tarts. Time to bake from twenty minutes to one and one-half hours. One quart of gooseberries, rather more than one-half pound of paste and sugar to taste. Remove the tops and tails from the gooseberries, or pick the currants from their stalks, or pare and core the apples; put them into a pie-plate with paste, pour a little water over it, put on a cover, ornament the edges in the usual manner and bake in a brisk oven.

## TARTLETS.

Bake one-quarter of an hour. Line patty-pans with puff paste, fill them with any kind of jam or preserve and bake lightly.

## OPEN JAM TART.

Bake until the paste loosens from the dish. Line a shallow tin dish with puff paste and put in the jam. Roll out some of the paste, wet lightly with the yolks of eggs beaten with a little milk and a tablespoonful of powdered sugar; cut it in narrow strips and place them across the tarts, lay another strip around the edge, trim off the outside and bake in a quick oven.

## ICED FRUITS FOR DESSERTS.

Any desirable fruit may be easily iced by dipping the fruit first into the beaten white of an egg, then into finely powdered sugar, again in the egg, sugar, and so on until it is of the desired thickness. For this purpose oranges or lemons should be carefully pared, and, as far as possible, all the inner white skin removed, to prevent a bitter taste. If lemons are used, cut in thin slices; if oranges, quarter. For cherries, strawberries, currants, etc., choose the largest and finest, leaving out the stems. Peaches should be pared and cut in halves. Sweet, juicy pears may be treated in the same manner, or look nicely when pared, leaving on the stems. Iced pineapple should be cut in thin slices and again divided into quarters.

### LEMON SHERBET OR ICE. Very nice.

One gallon of water and twelve lemons. Squeeze the lemon juice through a fine sieve. When the water nearly boils add the lemon juice. Take from the fire and put it into the freezer, freezing till hard; be careful and not let it freeze too hard. Have it a nice frosty color. Add sugar to sweeten very sweet.

### PINEAPPLE ICE.

This may be made like the lemon ice, only cut the pineapple in very small pieces. Put in the water and freeze. Add plenty of sugar.

### PEACH SHERBET OR ICE. Very delicate.

Twelve ripe or canned peaches and two quarts of water, sweeten to taste; add the juice of four or five lemons, put in the peaches and freeze as you would for lemon sherbet.

### RASPBERRY AND CURRANT ICES.

Proceed as for peach sherbet.

### FROZEN PUDDING.

Two cups of raisins, stemmed and stoned; the same quantity of peaches, two quarts of milk, sweeten to taste; add a little extract of vanilla. Put in peaches and raisins and one half box of Cox's gelatine; add to the milk when ready to freeze. Freeze, take out and put into moulds; pack in ice until ready to serve. Water can be used instead of milk, but if so, extract of lemon should be added in place of vanilla.

## ICE CREAMS.

There is often great difficulty in making good ice creams, either by too little flavoring, or too much freezing. Creams are sometimes made from boiled custard, and then again from milk and sweet cream, but in so doing corn starch should not be used, because when frozen it is liable to be too solid.

## VANILLA ICE CREAM.

Two quarts of sweet cream, sugar to sweeten very sweet, flavor with vanilla; freeze to a firm, hard cream. Draw off the water and repack with coarse salt and ice. Let it stand till ready to serve.

The writer thinks it necessary to mention the process of freezing, as some have the idea that all the water must be drawn off when freezing; but that is not necessary. When ready to freeze crack the ice as fine as possible and put it around the freezer, then a layer of salt, then another layer of ice, another layer of salt and so on until the freezer is full, not allowing it to reach the top as some might fall inside; then begin to freeze. When the ice begins to settle as it melts, draw off a little of the water to keep it from overflowing; then repack, and so on till done. When the cream is frozen sufficiently, take out the dasher, and pack with salt and ice as at first; be sure then to draw off all the water.

### VANILLA ICE CREAM. No. 2.

Put on two quarts of sweet milk to boil; add sugar to sweeten. When boiling add six beaten eggs, stirring continually. Remove from the fire and strain through a hair sieve. Flavor with vanilla, and freeze.

### COFFEE, CHOCOLATE AND LEMON ICE CREAM.

May be made in the same way. Strain in coffee to suit the taste, sweeten and freeze.

Chocolate—Grate the chocolate fine, moisten with water, strain, add to the cream and freeze.

Lemon—Flavor with extract of lemon and sweeten to taste.

### ORANGE ICE CREAM.

Two quarts of new cream, made very sweet with sugar. Pare and cut the oranges in small pieces; then add to the cream and freeze. Use eight or ten oranges to flavor nicely.

# GENERAL REMARKS ON JELLIES.

One package of Cox's gelatine; let it soak in water sufficient to cover it when soaked very soft. Let one quart of water come to a boil; then add the gelatine, two lemons and one-half pound of sugar; let this boil, then add the beaten whites of two eggs, stirring constantly till the eggs are cooked. Wet a flannel bag in warm water, that the gelatine may run through. Pour in the jelly, letting it run through slowly until the contents become clear; then empty the bag, wash and run through again. Put in moulds and set in a cool place to harden.

## WINE JELLY.

One package of Cox's gelatine, soak as in the above recipe; one pint of water, one cup of white wine, one lemon, one-half pound of granulated sugar, one stick of cinnamon and the whites of two eggs. Let the water come to a boil; then add the gelatine, sugar, cinnamon and lemon. After it has boiled about twenty minutes, add the beaten whites of eggs and cook until the eggs are done; take from the fire and add the wine; mix well, strain through a flannel bag twice. Put into moulds and set aside in a cool place to harden.

## JELLY MADE FROM THE STOCK POT. Aspic Jelly.

Take bones of beef or any fresh meat bones that are prepared for the stock pot, wash and trim off all the fat, cover with cold water and let it simmer on the back of the range about twenty-four hours. When it is boiled down about half, draw it off, put it into a porcelain pail and set away to cool; then skim off all the fat that rises on top. Dip out the jellied stock with a spoon so as not to get the settlings. Put it into a porcelain pail; flavor with cinnamon and one or two lemons, according to the quantity of stock, sweeten with granulated sugar; boil down slowly. Take the whites of two or three eggs beaten to a froth, adding them last, stir with a spoon until cooked. Take from the fire and strain through a flannel bag. The greatest failure in making jellies is to get them clear. They should be as clear as crystal. Be sure and not strain before the egg is thoroughly cooked, for in so doing the jelly will have a milky color. Sweet jellies can be made from stock as from crystalized gelatine, by flavoring and sweetening as in the foregoing recipes. Also to make from stock, boil it down and let cool, take off all the fat that rises on top; flavor with mace, cinnamon and celery. Boil about twenty minutes, season with salt and pepper, add the whites of eggs and strain through a flannel bag till clear. Serve with tongue or boned turkey. Salt and pepper should be used very light.

## RIBBON JELLY.

Soak one package of gelatine in cold water two or three hours. Boil one quart of water and add the juice of three lemons, one-half pound of sugar, a little cinnamon and one-half gill of white wine last; add the gelatine, dissolve and mix well. Take out about one-third of the liquor and put it into another dish; add two sheets of red gelatine or cochineal to give the pink color; then take another third of the liquor from the plain gelatine, and color purple with cochineal. Let the three boil gently about ten minutes, add the beaten whites of two eggs to each dish of liquid jelly and let them boil two minutes more. Have three separate jelly bags; strain and put the plain or wine jelly at the bottom of a quart mould; let this harden before adding the other color; when this is hard pour on the purple, then the pink after the purple is cold. When ready to serve, set the mould in a pan of warm water, that the jelly may slip from the mould easily. Turn into a glass dish. This makes a very pretty dish when properly made.

These recipes may look very simple, but when carefully practiced, will be found to be very nice, because they have all been tried by the writer.

## GENERAL REMARKS ABOUT CATERING.

To cater for parties or spreads we want to have a plenty, and not too much left over to be wasted. In so doing we must know the number of persons to be in the party, so as to make no mistake in buying the quantity of food to supply them. Always be sure to have plenty of solids or meat in the first course, so that when the desserts and fruits are put on the table they will soon have plenty, even though the fruits should fall short.

For a party of twenty five persons:—two cold boiled tongues, sliced thin; one boiled twelve pound ham, cold and sliced thin. This tongue and ham will give you all you will want for two medium sized platters. Also have three fowls, boiled, picked from the bones and chopped fine for chicken sandwiches; it will make from twenty-five to thirty. For lobster salad, take ten lobsters, pick from the shell and cut in small pieces. Two quarts of ice cream, three loaves of cake, one each of plain, citron and fruit; thirty bananas, twenty apples, three pints of cracked nuts and two quarts of strong coffee.

## CHICKEN SANDWICHES.

Chop the chicken very fine, then season with salt and pepper to taste. Mix a tablespoonful of dry mustard into two and one-half pounds of butter, then mix in the chicken. If it works stiff, add a very little warm water, enough to make a smooth paste that can be spread with a palette knife between the slices. Put the bread together, trim nicely and arrange on a dish for the table. The above bill of fare is suitable for either dinner or supper.

## BILL OF FARE.

For a party of twenty-five persons.
*Cold Tongue.*—Two medium sized.
*Cold Ham.*—One twelve pound ham.
*Chicken Sandwiches.*—Thirty.
*Lobster Salad.*—Ten or twelve lobsters.
*Ice Cream.*—Two quarts.
*Cake.*—One loaf each of plain, citron and itfru.
*Nuts.*—Mixed, three pints, cracked.
*Coffee.*—Two quarts.

## BILL OF FARE.

For a party of fifty persons.

*Soup.*—Tomato, four quarts.

*Fish.*—Boiled salmon, sixteen pounds.

*Removes.*—Roast ribs of beef, thirty pounds; chicken salad, three quarts; mashed potatoes, nine quarts; boiled sweet corn, eight cans.

*Dessert.*—Vanilla ice cream, eight quarts; bananas, fifty; mixed nuts, three quarts; coffee, two gallons.

This bill of fare, if carefully served, will be enough with some left over.

## DIRECTIONS FOR SETTING A TABLE.

To set a table in a dining room, plainly furnished without pictures on the wall, set the table as near the centre of the room as possible. It is customary to have a white linen cloth on the table, and there may be a plain red cloth in the centre, on which the castor is placed. Arrange the cups and soup in front of the lady of the house, while the meat and vegetables are placed before the master. Put a plate for each person, and a soup plate, also knife, fork and soup spoon. Have the pepper, salt and other relishes around the castor, if there is room. After the soup is disposed of, remove the tureen, soup plates and spoons, and bring in the meat and vegetables.

## DIRECTIONS FOR SETTING A TABLE. No. 2.

This is for twelve persons. You should have an experienced waiter or waitress to set the table and to pass the courses in the order mentioned. Set the table, fold the napkin for each person in a plain style, and put on crackers, water, glasses, pitcher and other things to make the table look nice. When it is time for dinner to be served, put on the soup. After the soup, bring in small fish plates, and serve the fish and potatoes. The meat and vegetables follow. Then remove all of the soiled dishes and put on clean plates, saucers and spoons for the dessert, with the coffee cups wine glasses and wine.

## BILL OF FARE. No. 1.

*Oysters.*—On half shell.

*Soup.*—Consomme royal.

*Fish.*—Boiled salmon, pommes de terre a la hollandaise.

*Boiled.*—Mutton, caper sauce.

*Removes.*—Roast rib of beef, dish gravy.

*Entrees.*—Fricassee chicken a la American.

*Cold Dishes.*—Boned turkey in jelly.

*Vegetables.*—Mashed new potatoes, boiled potatoes, stewed tomatoes.

88

*Pudding.*—English plum, brandy sauce.
*Pastry.*—Apple and mince pie.
*Dessert.*—Vanilla ice cream, assorted cake, fruits, nuts, raisins, cheese and crackers.
*Beverages.*—Tea and coffee.

## BILL OF FARE. No. 2.

*Soup.*—Mock turtle.
*Fish.*—Baked white fish, wine sauce, sliced tomatoes.
*Boiled.*—Sugar cured tongue, cider jelly.
*Roast.*—Rib of beef, yorkshire pudding; turkey, cranberry sauce.
*Game.*—Woodcock on toast.
*Entrees.*—Queen fritter, rum sauce.
*Cold Dishes.*—Corned beef, mutton,
*Vegetables.*—Boiled and mashed potatoes, succotash and string beans.
*Pudding.*—Tapioca in cream.
*Pastry.*—Apple custard pie.
*Dessert*—Lemon sherbet, sponge and marble cake, cheese, tea, coffee and crackers.
*Fruit.*—Grapes, raisins, oranges and cracked nuts.

## BILL OF FARE. No. 3.

*Soup.*—Scotch broth, beef.
*Fish.*—Boiled cusk, egg sauce; smelts in crumbs a la tartar, saratoga potatoes, lettuce and sliced tomatoes.
*Boiled.*—Chicken, white sauce; boiled corned beef and spinach. Sherry wine.
*Roast.*—Rib of beef, sirloin of beef, dish gravy; spring lamb, mint sauce.
Roman punch.
*Game.*—Wild turkey stuffed with chestnuts.
*Entrees.*—Baked chicken pie, family style, omelette souffle. Punch brandy (cognac.)
*Cold Dishes.*—Boned turkey in jelly.
*Puddings.*—English plum, wine sauce.
*Pastry.*—Apple and squash pies.
*Dessert.*—Strawberry ice cream, assorted cake, confectionery, cheese and pilot bread.
*Fruit.*—Oranges, bananas, apples, grapes and nuts.
*Beverages.*—Tea and coffee.

## BILL OF FARE. No. 4. Breakfast.

Oat meal, hominy. Beef steak, lamb chops, liver and bacon, ham and eggs. Fried cod. Ham omelette, onion omelette, boiled, scrambled and poached eggs. Parker house rolls, wheat gems, corn muffins, buckwheat cakes. Tea, coffee and cocoa in shells.

## BILL OF FARE. Luncheon.

Oyster stew, small tenderloin steak, cold biscuits and pickled lamb's tongues. Tea.

## BILL OF FARE. No. 5. Dinner.

*Soup.*—Clam chowder, small oyster patties.
*Boiled.*—Fresh pork and cabbage.
*Roast.*—Chicken, giblet sauce; spring lamb, mint sauce.
*Entrees.*—Baked macaroni and cheese.
*Pastry.*—Squash and dried apple pies.
*Dessert.*—Pound cake, fruit cake, frosted blanc mange, Catawba grapes, Oolong tea, coffee and mild cheese.

This bill of fare is suitable for Wednesday's or Friday's dinner.

## BILL OF FARE. No. 6,

*Soup.*—Mutton with rice.
*Boiled.*—Phila. capon a la creme.
*Roast.*—Rib of beef, dish gravy; stuffed chicken, giblet sauce. Roman Punch.
*Entrees.*—Escalloped oysters, beefsteak smothered in onions.
*Cold Dishes.*—Sardines with lemons.
*Vegetables.*—Baked sweet potatoes, boiled white potatoes, rice and tomatoes.
*Pudding.*—Rice with sweet cream.
*Pastry.*—Lemon and cocoanut pies.
*Dessert.*—Vanilla ice cream, angel cake, lady cake and mild cheese.
*Fruit.*—Apples, oranges, mixed nuts and raisins.
*Confectionery.*—Conversation lozenges, chocolate candy.
*Beverages.*—Acorn coffee, Oolong tea.

## BREAKFAST MENU. No. 7.

Oat meal, hominy, corn meal and griddle cakes.
*Broils.*—Liver and bacon, ham, honeycomb tripe, sirloin steak and tenderloin beefsteak.
*Fish.*—Broiled schrod, fried cod, fried smelts and salmon steak. Ham and eggs, bacon and eggs.
*Eggs.*—Boiled, fried, poached, scrambled and dropped.
*Vegetables*—French fried potatoes, Saratoga chips, lyonaise and stewed potatoes.
*Bread.*—White, graham, wheat muffins, breakfast rolls, Vienna bread.
*Beverages.*—English breakfast tea, mixed tea, chocolate, cocoa in shells, Mocha and Java coffee.

This bill of fare may appear large for a family, but articles may be selected from it for a breakfast dish. This is a regular hotel bill of fare.

# FOR THE SICK, BURNS, ETC.

## BEEF TEA.

Wash, and cut off all the fat and rind from one pound of lean beef; place in a sauce pan and cover with cold water; let it simmer slowly on the back part of the stove for two hours; take off and strain, add a very small pinch of salt. Serve hot or cold.

## EGG SOUP.

Take two cups of chicken or veal broth. Skim off all the fat that may rise on top. Beat two raw eggs into it. Strain, and serve; or take one hard boiled egg, cut fine, and add. Season with salt and pepper. Sometimes a little mutton broth with rice is good, when made nicely.

## BRAXTON A LA CREAME.

One cup of mutton broth, or chicken; one-half stalk of celery cut in small pieces; two tablespoonsful of sweet cream; one half ounce of chicken cut fine; the beaten yolk of one egg. When the broth is cooked, add the ingredients mentioned, and one and one-half tablespoonsful of cooked rice, and one hard boiled egg, chopped fine. Season to taste with salt and pepper. You will find this to be a very delicate and strengthening dish for the sick.

## FOR CONSUMPTIVE PERSONS.

Six or seven leaves of mullen, steeped in milk, sweetened, and taken before going to bed, is said to be very good.

## FOR BURNS AND SCALDS.

Apply sweet oil, flour and molasses mixed.

Oat and Graham Meal Gruels are very good for the sick. Cook one-half cup of oat-meal in milk; strain through a strainer, and serve.

Ginger tea is said to be very good for cramps. Boil two table-spoonsful of ginger in milk; sweeten with sugar. Take hot.

To be a practical and competent cook, you will need to try and learn to do as those tell you who have had many years experience.

Those who desire to learn the art of cooking, to day, will find it much easier than I did; because at the time when I commenced there were no cooking schools where I could obtain instruction from competent teachers, as many young men and women do now.

No matter how long you may have been cooking, you may learn something new every day in this art, as in any other work. There are many dishes gotten up by cooks that have not been published; so you may see, in a new published cook book, something never thought of by the reader.

Some think that because they are not of French or German birth it is impossible to become skilful cooks or bakers, but this is a great mistake. It makes no difference of what nationality you are, if you only put your mind and attention to the art.

This is probably the first cook book of the kind ever published by a colored chef ; but when you have read it carefully, and studied the recipes, you will find something as good as foreign cooks could make.

I shall always remember the words of an old cook whom I worked under, who said: "the American people did not take sufficient interest in cooking, but cooking was one of the keys to civilization."

I sincerely hope that the young people of America will learn the art and skill of cooking, as the young men and women of England and other foreign countries have done.

GEO. F. BRAXTON, *Author*.

# GENERAL INDEX.